LIVES THAT OFT REMIND US

By

Enos Kincheloe Cox

Gloster, Miss.

Author of *Christian Stewardship,*
"Where Is the Lord God of Elijah?"
The Answer By Fire, etc.

CHICAGO

THE BIBLE INSTITUTE COLPORTAGE ASS'N

843–845 North Wells Street

PRINTED IN THE UNITED STATES OF AMERICA

To My Beloved Wife

AILEEN GALLOWAY COX

"Honor, anger, valor, fire;
A love that life could never tire,
Death quench or evil stir,
The mighty Master gave to her.

"Teacher tender, comrade, wife,
A fellow-farer true through life;
Heart whole and soul free
The august Father gave to me."

FOREWORD

FROM early boyhood the accounts of the men and women of the Old Testament have had a very great fascination for me. I was taught to know and love them by a consecrated grandmother and a sister of my mother who lived with the family when I was beginning to read. They taught me to read those stories, and the interest which was aroused has remained until now.

The record of those lives was preserved that we might learn how God dealt with them, and know that humanity all down the centuries has had the same weaknesses and virtues, the same temptations and triumphs; has encountered the same enemies, and found strength and deliverance as the faithful find it today.

Those people of the long ago were intensely human; their faults were like our faults, and their joys and sorrows very much the same as our own. It is gloriously worth while to us that we study their experiences and discover from these wonderful glimpses of their lives how God has striven through all history to reveal Himself to our race.

E. K. C.

CONTENTS

9

Abel

THE FIRST OF THE REDEEMED

E VER since sin came into the world, children have brought both joy and sorrow. It was so in the first home of earth and will be so till the end.

We are told that Eve seemed to feel that her first-born would be the fulfillment of the pristine promise made just before she and her husband were driven out of Eden. Little did she dream of the long trail of tears and blood ere that promise would become a reality. Cain, the beloved and hope-centered first-born, brought grief and heartbreak too deep for words, and made known to Eve, in some measure at least, the awful things which sin would mean to the race.

No one can explain why one of the two boys in that first home should go wrong—awfully and irretrievably wrong! Sin lurks like a deadly virus in the blood of the race, and sometimes breaks out in full force where it is least expected. Somehow, the full measure of the rebellious spirit that brought sin into the world came to repleteness in the life of Cain. These brothers were taught the worship of Jehovah, and in some manner the idea of the sacrifice of a substitute for sin was made known to them. The first family was a worshipping family, and when the sons came to manhood they brought their offerings to Jehovah.

In the sacrifice of Cain we see the beginning of the long line of those who have sought to make themselves acceptable to the most High by the works of their hands. They have always said: "My own works, my own deeds are good enough, and God ought to be pleased that I have brought Him that which I have made."

It was different with Abel. From some source there had come into his heart a real concept of the thing which we call sin, and he realized that all he might do would be imperfect. He had doubtless meditated on the promise of the One who should bruise the head of the serpent, and realized that in bruising him that One would suffer death. The idea of atonement was dim and misty, but Abel knew that things were not right between him and God, and he knew that sin meant death. How much he understood about those things we can only conjecture. We are told, however, that it was "by faith" that he offered "a more excellent sacrifice than Cain"; so he must have looked beyond the bleeding lamb that smoked upon his altar, and hoped for something that God would do that would really take away his sin.

It is a grandly pathetic picture, this son of earth without a Bible, with only the faint promise of something to come, bringing his offering of a substitute and laying it before God as a satisfaction for his sin. It was a groping faith and for that reason more divinely beautiful.

Two Altars; Two Worshippers

Let us look for a moment at those two altars and their worshippers. One of them stood proudly erect before his altar on which burned the fruits of his labors, looking as though he had given enough and expecting the approval of God. The other altar was stained with blood, bearing a body which had lately throbbed with life; and the penitent who knelt beside it looked through the flame and smoke with the most intense expectancy. In that face were mingled sorrow and joy—sorrow for sin and joy that saw the time when God would fulfill His promise and in mercy take away the guilty stains. Abel's offering said: "I am a sinner and I deserve to die, but here is my offering and it pleads God's promise; sin calls for death but this substitute has died in my place; I now believe that in His own appointed way God forgives and forgets my sins according to His promise."

Abel was the first evangelical; he was the progenitor of the line which sought for mercy; he brought an offering of blood, believing that God had provided a way for the remission of his sins.

What a portrait of faith! A lone man with no Bible, no prophet or teacher; with only the memory of a promise which his parents had told him in fear and trembling! He did not fully understand but he believed God, and in the light of that flame saw the face of a reconciled Father. But Cain was seeking the pre-eminence, he wanted the leadership of the family; the spirit that would rather rule in hell than serve in heaven blazed in him, and he determined that he would have his own way despite both God and Abel. We know the outcome! When Cain saw that Abel was preferred he slew his brother, that he might not be in his way.

Abel was dead, the first of that mighty company who have suffered because they stood in the way of evil and the ambitions of wicked men. That first cold body was picked up by the broken-hearted parents, and laid in the first grave digged by human hands. Adam and Eve were drinking the cup of bitterness which was pressed from the sin which had broken the tie that bound them to God. What a group that was about the foremost grave of earth! Shame, wonder and bitter heartache were there. Adam looked on with tearless eyes, filled with brooding horror. Eve wept as mothers have wept down the ages, and pondered the promise that seemed broken or pushed into the dim distance. Cain sulked in the background with shame and bitter thoughts of self-exculpation.

How hopeless, drab and drear it all seemed! And the same thing has been re-enacted millions of times in the ages since. Sin had appeared as only a little thing, a tiny trickle not worth noticing; but in the cruel grief and despair about that grave, we see the prophecy of the flood of shame and guilt which would mantle the world and shadow the hearts of the entire race.

"O Grave, Where Is Thy Victory?"

Yet there was light and hope in that grave, if we understand it aright. Sin had digged its first sepulchre, but the first man to sleep in the bosom of mother earth was a man of faith. The first soul to slip out of its tenement of clay went to heaven. Was there not in that grave a promise of the time when redeemed humanity shall sing of their victory over death, as they will look upon the risen Christ, alive forevermore? Doubtless no such thought crossed the mind of Adam and Eve, but the promise stood, and that first grave was an earnest of the mighty host of God's children who have gone that way to heaven since then.

Abel was gone, but God had him in His keeping. Cain sought to put him out of his way, but murder never gets the victim out of the murderer's way. Not only was the blood of Abel crying its crimson accusation into the ear of God, but Abel was forever safe in the place from which Cain sought to expel him. Abel was for all time the pioneer of that victorious multitude whom John saw, as told in the seventh chapter of Revelation. Abel now leads that uncounted and uncountable host which are robed in white garments, washed in the blood of the Lamb, of whom his lamb foretold.

He was the first child of faith, the foremost to grasp that loftiest truth of revelation, namely, that men must come to God through some expiation for sin made by some One other than sinful man. He was the earliest to lie down in earth's solitary tomb; the leader of those who pass through the gates of death into the rest that remaineth for the people of God. He was the first martyr to the envy and malice of the forces of evil. He was the leader of the long roll of witnesses who sealed their faith with their blood. The roster of those heroes of faith who have lived and wrought, suffered and died is the most illustrious of all time. They are a company concerning whom we are told that "the world was not worthy"; and at the head of that long procession stands the figure and the name of Abel, the righteous son of the first human family.

There are many places where a man or his name may be honored. Every country cherishes the memory of its distinguished sons and daughters who have shed luster upon its history. They are counted worthy to have their names and deeds wrought into imperishable memorials for the inspiration and guidance of future generations. America has its statuary hall in the very heart of our country. Britain has her Westminster Abbey. Other nations have their shrines equally sacred to them, which tell like stories. But none of them has a roll so ancient, so glorious and lasting as the one headed by the name of Abel. He was the first of the redeemed, the first to testify with blood to the faith which was "once for all delivered to the saints."

The First Man to Enter Heaven

One cannot but wonder about Abel going to heaven. We are told that the angels desire to look into the glory of the plan of redemption. We are also told that "the morning stars sang together, and the sons of God shouted for joy," as they welcomed the new world which God had made. There must have been more than ordinary interest when the foremost one of the redeemed children of the wayward race came to dwell with that beatific company. A new song began in heaven with only one voice, a song which should echo through ages yet unborn. How all heaven must have listened! Here was a song unheard before, a melody set to the chord of redeeming love. How it must have thrilled that unsinning host! They might admire its sweetness and beauty, but not one of them could join in it. They had not known sin; they had not felt its defilement; they had never trembled under its guilt, nor experienced its removal by the redeeming blood of the sacrifice. They could only listen in silent awe and admiring wonder!

Abel must have been a bit lonely at first. There was none in heaven with that same experience, none who knew the depths into which man had fallen, or who could share the heavenly thrills and the divine ecstasy which come with pardon and deliverance. However, as others came and that hallelujah chorus grew with the passing centuries, it must have seemed more and more wonderful to Abel. Since then, he has seen the company of the redeemed increase until they surpass the stars for multitude; and the melody of that choir has grown in volume until no other music in the heavenlies is comparable with it. A glorious volume might be written about the heavenly experiences of Abel.

Abel was the first of the earthborn to die. His body filled the first grave hollowed out by human hands. He was the earliest of all to crimson the soil with his life-blood, and the file leader of the line of God's martyred saints to enter the city that hath foundations. The first altar that offered acceptable sacrifice was built by his hands, and the holy City heard from his ransomed spirit the first notes of that song of redemption, the new song which shall never cease. Abel has welcomed all the uncounted company which have gone through the gates with singing to their eternal abode.

There is some sort of prophecy in the life and death of Abel. It was no accident that the first man to die went to heaven. It whispers a message of resplendent victory over death and sin that the first victim of death went to be with God, and that the one whose body shall rise from the oldest grave of earth shall come in the glory of an eternal triumph.

It looked like righteousness was defeated and that sin was a conqueror when Cain stood with cruel club over the cold form of the first man to serve God aright; but in the light of the long cycles truth stands triumphant, Abel has conquered, and his line is made up of the victors of the ages who have overcome through the blood of the Lamb and "loved not their lives unto the death."

Abel is the primal pledge of redemption, the lone martyr of the dark days when sin seemed to have won the fight. He is now numbered the chief and foremost among the conquerors, and the leader of that army which has won through death unto life everlasting.

References: Genesis 4:1–15, 25; Luke 11:49–51; Hebrews 11:4; 12:24.

Enoch

GOD'S COMRADE

THERE are just four verses in the Bible about Enoch, and yet they have made his name immortal. He has come down to us as the man who walked with God in the darkest days this world has known, and who just walked on until God took him to be with Himself forever.

Walking is not a spectacular thing; it is rather prosaic to most people. Running and flying create interest, and cause crowds to gather. No one would go to the races if the horses walked around the track; but Enoch got especial mention on the honor roll of the faithful by just walking all the time in the right direction.

Enoch lived in those dark days before the deluge when the race was hastening toward its watery doom. Sin was covering the earth like a midnight pall and the face of God was hidden. All flesh was becoming corrupt, and the evil imaginations of the mighty men were filling the earth with violence.

It is refreshing to know that in such a day there was a man who had full and complete fellowship with God. No man in the divine record has a more beautiful encomium than that which the Holy Spirit passed upon this man who lived amid the thickening shadows.

We find that his walking with God began when he was sixty-five years old, and we wonder at first why it should have begun at that particular time. We begin to understand when we read that at that age a son came to bless his home. When Enoch looked into the face of his first born, the world changed for him. He knew the sort of world in which his boy must live, and that it would take all possible good influences to keep him amid the surrounding evil. So Enoch took stock; he looked within to see what sort of man he was, and he wondered what kind of man his boy would be were he to become like his father. It is likely that he said, "I have brought an immortal life into this world, and for that life I am responsible; I must be a good man." Somewhere in a secret place things were settled, and Enoch became God's man.

Walking With God

We know a man by the company that he keeps, and when we read of Enoch that "he walked with God," we begin to know this man. What a word: "Walked with God!" Walking is a very common thing; it belongs to the plodding everyday affairs of life. It means that in all the ordinary affairs of daily routine that Enoch and God were together. Not only during the important hours of his life but in the simple matters of each day, he communed with God. When Enoch went to the field or his place of labor, God was there; and when he came home at noon, God was there. When the shades of evening mantled the earth, God and Enoch talked things over; and through the darkness, the One who never sleeps was by his side. When he opened his eyes in the morning, he heard the voice of God and his soul was conscious of His presence. It was no flimsy, flabby sort of piety which made the life of Enoch clean and beautiful, but the constant fellowship with Him who is the embodiment of all that is pure and holy.

We do not know much of the worship of those far off days, but we do know that in all ages men and women who loved God have gathered to worship Him. We may be sure that Enoch was found among that ancient company wherever they met. His religion did not begin when he entered the place of worship; neither did it cease when he went away. Enoch did not go there to meet God; God was with him all the time, but he went there for fellowship.

The folk all had confidence in Enoch, though there were some who said he was too strait-laced and narrow. Enoch did not go where his great Companion was not welcome; and we know that when a man's life stands the test of the presence of God, he is not going to be popular with some people.

For a long time Jesus was not a popular preacher. As long as He fed the crowd, they wanted to make Him king; but when He set forth the truth of spiritual living that causes separation from the world, they left Him as men flee from a pestilence. So we should not think of Enoch as a man whom everybody praised, but as one who in the darkest days of the world dared to be out and out for God. The reign of lust and cruelty which caused the Almighty to wipe the slate clean for a new start was under way, and godliness was not in favor with the mind of the crowd.

Enoch had settled some things, and it is a masterful achievement to be able to settle the real affairs of life. The man who walks with God must walk straight. The highway of holiness is not a wide and meandering path. Only the latitudinarians are good company for the careless, pleasure-loving multitude. A lot of trouble comes from the people who know the right, but love the favor of the rabble too well to displease anybody. Enoch had to walk across many of the customs and usages of his day. The world was on the down grade, and the man who walked with God would have little human company. Walking with God was not easy for Enoch; it is not easy now, and never will be in this world of sin; but the end will be glorious.

Going God's Way

"Enoch walked with God." That means that he went God's way, for God does not change. It means that he cut loose from the world and gave over the reins of his life to God. The path in which men walk with God has no left turns, and we cannot choose the way when we walk with Him. He must decide, not just part of the time, but all the time. "In all thy ways acknowledge Him," said the inspired writer. These things are not as easy to perform as they sound. It takes iron in the blood to walk like Enoch and not turn aside. To withstand the sneers and innuendoes of a degenerate and God-hating world demands the real stuff of genuine manhood. To be "good" in the Bible sense of that word is testing work, and many of us are too weak in fiber to be good. Anybody can run with the gang and frolic in the devil's playgrounds, but to say "No" all the while to the lusty calls of the flesh and the siren voice of pleasure, one must have the moral muscle of the trained spiritual athlete. Enoch was no weakling, but one who could choose for himself and, leaving the crowd, walk in the way that God blazed out for him.

Enoch was often lonely on the human side of his life, but what company he had! A man is mightily shaped by the company he keeps. The fact that he walked with God does not mean that he was all the time conscious of God's presence, for God sometimes leaves His chosen ones to struggle in the dark, that they may learn to walk by faith and not by sight. Sometimes He hides Himself, even as our Lord with the disciples on the way to Emmaus. It was often so with Enoch, but he just kept going in the way that He knew God was going. That is the art of walking with God, just going His way. God is going in the way of holiness, in the paths of love, mercy and justice; and He dwells with him that is of a humble and contrite spirit, and trembleth at His word.

We learn from Enoch that one can walk with God under all circumstances and against all odds. The world has not known a darker day than that in which Enoch lived with shining face and spotless life. All the customs and habits of the world about him led away from God and right, but he withstood the temptations of the worst era that the world has known. There was every call of the flesh which we know, the allurement of every selfish ambition, and the clamor of the crowd; yet in spite of it all, he lifted his face toward the heights, and walked and talked with the King.

We are often tempted to repine and say that the way is hard, and that it is not possible to live the Christ-life in our day. It will do us good to take a long look at this sturdy saint—without a Bible, a church or a prophet-friend—trudging on the Godward way and walking unfalteringly to the end. Jude tells that Enoch was a prophet, and that he looked down the long, intervening ages and saw the coming of the King with His saints. A man who walks with God gets the long-look, and centuries and millenniums do not mean much in the purposes of God.

The End of the Way

This life had a wonderful close. Such lives do not have to change directions; the course is the same for time and for eternity. Enoch was walking in the way of life and death missed him, for death is not found along the way which he walked. One day he disappeared from among his fellows. There was no death-bed, no funeral, no burial, but the man was gone. He walked out with God one day and never came back, and those who knew him best said that God had taken him. The people knew where Enoch had gone; they knew which way he had been walking for three hundred years; and when they saw him last, he was walking that way.

The Bible says, "He was not, for God took him." He was not in his home; he was not in his place of business, nor in the place of worship. Enoch was ripe for heaven, and did not have to wait for death to take him by way of the grave. He was just walking on with God, and God said: "Enoch, we are going home"; and I think Enoch answered: "All right, Lord, I have been wanting to go for a long time; this old world is getting worse and worse, and I am tired of its sin and evil ways; I am ready."

The Joy of Translation

So the Lord and Enoch walked on together, and he was in heaven before he knew it. Where is Enoch? He is where all men go who walk with God. We know some people have gone to heaven because they left earth headed that way, and directions do not change on the other side. If you want to find out where anyone went when he left this world, just find out the way he was headed when he left the earth. Enoch did not have any death-bed repenting to do; he did not have to change the course of his life when the shadows began to fall. He just walked on with his Lord, and the journey ended inside the gates of the city where there is no night.

I think that Enoch was glad to go. The world was growing worse and worse, and fast becoming ripe for the doom of the deluge. His soul was weary of the crimes of those mighty sinners, who delighted in all sorts of violence, and he was homesick for his own country.

Just what it means to be translated no one knows. The Bible does not explain some things; it simply says that he did "not see death." Enoch did not pass through the experience which all men have suffered since the beginning, except Elijah, and it is not wise to speculate beyond what is written. Just how it happened and what changes took place are wisely kept from us, but Enoch must have made some marvelous attainments in sainthood in order to have this wonderful privilege. He may have gone home like Elijah, escorted by heavenly chariots of flaming light, or there may have been no unusual manifestations. This much we know, that God took him, and he did not pass through the gloomy valley of the shadow of death. He stands as an example of the triumphs of grace and holiness, over against the darkness of those days when God was forgotten and sin seemed to have conquered the human race.

If one could live such a life in such a time, what ought we to do who have the knowledge of Christ and the background of centuries of Christian history? Enoch stands as a constant rebuke to those of us who plead the times in which we live, and the temptations which beset us as an excuse for our sorry living. It is a joy to look back across the intervening ages and see this crystal character with its beauty and strength testifying to the power of God that gives triumph over the worst environment and the most trying temptations the world has known. God has had His witnesses in every age, but there is something of peculiar wonder and beauty in this life of Enoch. It sheds its light across the awful cataclysm of the deluge; it gleams through the days of the law and the prophets; and in the greater revelations of the Christian era, it stands as a paragon of what the grace of God can do for a human soul.

We shall see Enoch one of these days and hear him tell of that wonderful journey. He will tell us how he walked with God against all the currents of that age, until one day he walked into that glory which shall be revealed to us also at the coming of our Lord.

Sublime character of the misty past! Grand old man of the pre-deluvian days! God's mighty prophet who kept the faith and walked in holiness in the midst of corruption, and went home unscathed by the sting of death! Let us catch some of the glory that gleams from this life athwart the ages, and get fresh courage from that shining face as we watch it pass from the darkness into the clouds which veil the abiding place of light.

References: Genesis 5:18–24; Hebrews 11:5; Jude 14–16.

Mrs. Noah

AN OLD TIME PREACHER'S WIFE

I**T IS** just a bit embarrassing to write about a woman who is
related to everybody whom you meet. We all recognize
the fact that we are sons and daughters of mother Eve, but
forget the fact that the same is true concerning our mother,
Mrs. Noah. In fact, our kinship to her is closer by several
generations. If to be the mother of a long and numerous
line entitles one to distinction, then Mrs. Noah goes next to
the head of the class. Mother Eve is first by seniority, but
our heroine is a close second.

We do not know the name of this remarkable woman,
where she was born, where she lived, or where she died. We
are told nothing of her ancestry, and very little of her personal
life. But we do know that she lived in a tragic era, an age
of violence and crime beyond any other the world has known.
She lived at a time when the world forgot God, and she
witnessed that unparalleled manifestation of divine power
known as the Deluge. She saw God wipe the slate clean for
a new start with the race, and He used her and hers as the
starters.

The world which the flood buried must have been a busy,
densely populated world, filled with many evidences of human
achievements. We are told by scientists that the Cro-Magnon
man, whose remains are found in many places, was superior to
our present race in size of body and brain capacity. Is it
not reasonable to conclude that these might be those of whom
Holy Writ says, "There were giants in the earth in those

days; . . . the same became mighty men which were of old, men of renown" (Gen. 6:4)? It is foolish to think that these people were what we call savages. Maybe the legend of the lost Atlantis and others of similar nature have their roots back in pre-deluvian times. However that may be, Mrs. Noah had a most wonderful experience in passing from that world, teeming with men and women in their crowded cities, into the new world of solitude and death.

Mrs. Noah was the wife of a busy, hard-working preacher. Peter tells us that Noah was a preacher of righteousness. According to the record, all the world is descended from this one preacher's wife. Many things have been written and said about the faithfulness and courage of father Noah, but mother Noah lived at the same time and under the same conditions, and I am saying a good word for her.

I am persuaded that she was a woman of piety and great strength of character, for no woman who was not made of more than ordinary stuff could have passed through those trying days and remained true to God. To go to some lonely altar for worship, when every other woman in the world went with the throngs to the gorgeous temples of idolatry, and to meet the sneers and ostracism which must have been her lot were severe tests of loyalty. The forms of evil were made attractive, for people lived long and had time to perfect and carry out their plans. The social set, the elite and the antedeluvian "four hundred" lifted their penciled eyebrows when someone mentioned that preacher's wife who was so terribly behind the times.

It was just as awful to be out of step then as it is now. No doubt many of the things which we call new were known to them, but were lost in that great catastrophe. Sports, games, amusements that fed the lusts of the flesh, social life that was glamorous and seductive—all called to Mrs. Noah, but she stood the test and was not conformed to the world. The cry, "Everybody is doing it," did not catch her; she was too wise for that. If to be right when multitudes go wrong, if to be loyal when mighty throngs beckon to the broad way puts one on the honor roll of the heroes of faith, then Mrs. Noah has a place near the head of the list.

Trials of a Preacher's Wife

Her husband was a preacher, but mighty few people came to hear him preach; and he preached one hundred and twenty years without a convert. Preachers get mighty blue sometimes at best, but just think how it must have been with Noah! What a time mother Noah had with him during those long years! Somewhere in heaven there is a special retreat for preachers' wives, for they will need a good long rest before they can enjoy heaven as they should. They have for long years been the bumpers between their husbands and the world. Some folk say the preacher lives with his head in the clouds. The true preacher does more than that: his head must be above the clouds that he may see God's face and hear His voice, so that he may give His message to the multitude below. The preacher must live in the place of the things which are not seen, or he will mean very little to this poor old world living in the realm of things which are seen.

Now this is where the preacher's wife comes in and where Mrs. Noah shined. Noah became much discouraged sometimes. He was the only preacher that God had in the whole prodigal, unrepenting world. The people were paying no attention to his message, and no preacher likes to be unnoticed. Also Noah was doing a very foolish thing in the eyes of most people in building that immense, odd-looking ark.

What sport those fellows must have had about his dry-land

ship! The street corner, grocery store and drink-dive gang soon exhausted their topics of conversation, and then spent the rest of the time making up wisecracks about Noah and his coming flood. When Noah came home at night, it was Mrs. Noah who encouraged him, took the sting out of the bitter hurts, and sent him out again rested and full of confidence.

A preacher's wife bears the side of his life which the public does not see. They see him at his best in his hours of inspiration and power. They look upon him uplifted by some great theme, pouring forth words of exhortation, weaving eloquent sentences, comforting and cheering the multitudes. They meet him in their homes—the genial guest, the careful counsellor, the sympathizer in sorrow. She sees him in his hours of reaction—tired, cast down, sometimes cross and impatient—ready, like Elijah, to hunt a juniper tree and quit.

There is many a week during which the preacher's wife has cooked the meals, scrubbed the floors, washed the dishes, cared for the babies, mended big and little garments, darned socks, overseen the servants—if she was fortunate enough to have any—and kept the children out of the study, that his distracted brain might function. She has kept out intruders, entertained wearisome callers, answered telephone calls, and spent a long time trying to pacify Sister Sensitive, whose platitudinous feelings have been hurt. She has talked with persistent agents, who longed for pastoral endorsement for their wares, and has led the missionary society, toiling to infuse new life and stimulate flagging zeal.

All this and more she has done without pomp or parade, with no blast of trumpets or hum of approving voices. Some times she goes over his sermons, criticises and amends, though this is not made public. At last, Sunday comes and the preacher brings the product of heart and brain in a message of beauty and power. The people are delighted and praise their gifted pastor. They shower him with compliments and admiration, while the wife remains unnoticed in the background. The recording angel listens, yawns, heaves a sigh, and picks out a bigger and brighter star for the crown of the preacher's wife. It would be mighty interesting to read some of the items on the credit side of heaven's ledger.

The duties of the wife of the modern preacher are heavy enough, but I maintain that the woman who stood by a preacher through one hundred and twenty fruitless years and did not falter was surely someone worth remembering.

Mrs. Noah had no congenial associates, not even a Missionary Society or a Ladies Aid, where she might talk things over. She just told her troubles to the Lord, brushed up Noah's clothes, and looked after Shem, Ham and Japheth. This was her world—her husband, her boys and her God. Some would have thought that a very narrow life, but Mrs. Noah kept busy, kept the faith, lived a long time, and went home to heaven.

A Faithful Mother Rewarded

Mrs. Noah did a good job with her boys. She had the best boys in the world. God kept them when all the rest were drowned. It looked as if God wanted to give the lie to that hoary falsehood that preachers' boys are the worst in the country by putting it on record that the only boys worth saving when He drowned the world were the sons of a preacher. I commend Mrs. Noah to the consideration of those who complain that they have no control over their children. There were no good children in the world with whom they might play, no neighbor's home where they might go without encountering evil, but this preacher's wife kept her boys for God and the future.

The cheap, pleasure-loving crowd of her day called Mrs. Noah a kill-joy, and her children were not invited to the social functions of that period. Probably Shem, Ham and Japheth chafed a bit like children do today under such discipline, but when the flood came and the ark floated off, they were inside. Mother Noah was not an expert bridge player; she did not win any prizes in the games of chance; her name was not mentioned as the woman who wore the most startling gown at one of those functions where they flirted with other women's husbands and did not go home till morning. However, when the last survivor of that crowd had been swept from the loftiest mountains, her boys were safe.

No, you are mistaken, brother Noah did not train those boys; there never was a man who could do it single-handed. Besides, Noah had his preaching to do, and that ark to build, and could not give those boys the time they needed. Any one who reads the story with care and knows human nature will give Mrs. Noah full credit.

The time of the flood was hard upon Mrs. Noah. How she must have pined for a settled home again, while she floated around penned up with all those animals! What an experience when they went out of the ark into an empty world to begin a new race! How strange and still the world seemed, and how near God must have been to them!

The Grandmother of Our Generation

Mrs. Noah behaved well after the flood. She was the oldest woman in the world, and they all looked up to her and asked her advice. What a time she must have had with those grandchildren! What stories she could tell them of the world before the flood! No other grandmother in all time ever had such stories to tell to the younger generation. How they must have begged for tales of her experiences before and during that awful flood! It was worth while to have a grandmother who could tell them such things about what had happened to the world and why they happened.

We are told when Noah died but not Mrs. Noah; she may have outlived him. There is not so much told about his work after the flood; his work was largely done; there was not so much thrill in preaching to that little company of his descendants. The old preacher got into trouble when he mixed other things with his preaching. He became a horti-culturalist and experimented with grapes. He made wine, and whether he was ignorant about wine or underestimated his capacity, we do not know; but the old preacher got drunk, made a fool of himself and got his son Ham into trouble. We are not told what Mrs. Noah said, but rather think she put him to bed to sleep it off, and bathed his throbbing head the morning after. I do not think that Noah meant to get drunk, but his case is a warning to preachers not to wander into strange fields in their old age.

Just a parting glance at the career of Mrs. Noah. She was born before the Deluge and so lived, as it were, in two worlds. She was the wife of the only preacher that God had in those days, when a ruined and debauched world was stag-gering to its doom. She stood faithfully by her preacher-husband, when he was crushed many times by the futility of his preaching to a race that had forgotten God. Together they faced the scorn and open contempt of those one hundred and twenty years.

Mrs. Noah took care of the preacher, kept his home, looked after his children, and inspired his heart. It is the one who meets the active struggle of life that becomes cast down. The man who can fight and win like Elijah upon Mount Carmel, can also sit under a Juniper tree and want to die, and be just as sincere at one time as the other. Many an evening Noah came home ready to quit, but after a few hours with her cheerful spirit, he was once more ready for the fray.

A preacher has a hard time being a hero to his hard-working, patient wife. She sees him all the time at close range. You can get too close to a mountain to see it. You only get glimpses of the rugged rocks, steep cliffs and ravines —the things of the ugly surface. You have to get away from the mountain, ten, twenty and sometimes fifty miles, to stand awed before its majestic proportions. It is the same with men; it takes the view of time and distance to measure them. Mr. and Mrs. Noah were both big folk; they still loom large on the far away centuries. He was a sure-enough preacher, and she was just an old-fashioned preacher's wife. I do not think they ever thought of being remarkable folk—they were too busy. Mrs. Noah became the first woman of the new earth by just being true to the great, simple things of life: her God, her husband, and her children, and these duties made up her daily round. She gave her best to her husband, and they floated off together to found a new world. She gave her best to her boys, and they were chosen from the ruined world to be God's seed corn for a better one.

So there was a time when the greatest woman in the world was a preacher's wife, and if our eyes were opened to see aright, some of them may be still. We do know, however, that many of them belong, like Mrs. Noah, to that company of whom "the world was not worthy."

References: Genesis 5:24; Genesis, chapters 6, 7, 8, 9; Matthew 24:37–39; Hebrews 11:7; I Peter 3:20; II Peter 2:5.

Abraham

PIONEER FOR GOD

NEARLY four thousand years ago, God called a man known as Abram of Ur in Chaldea to leave his native land and journey to a country which He would show him. Abram obeyed God and went out, not knowing where he was going. His wife and Lot, his brother's son, were the only relatives who shared his pilgrimage.

The call of this man and his obedience are epochal in the religious history of the world. Possibly, no single emigrant of all time meant so much to the future of humanity. Abram, whose name was changed to Abraham, was born among the heathen people of Chaldea, and his early life was spent among those who had low and material concepts of Deity. There came to him in this darkness a vision of God as the invisible, spiritual, holy and eternal One. Just how this truth was first made known to Abraham we do not know, but the revelation came and he was not disobedient to the heavenly vision. Of his early life the record is silent. He comes under our observation when God called him from his native land and he obeyed, "not knowing whither he went."

The promise which was made him was world-wide and time-lasting in its scope: "And I will make of thee a great nation, and I will bless thee, and make thy name great; and thou shalt be a blessing: and I will bless them that bless thee, and curse him that curseth thee: and in thee shall all families of the earth be blessed" (Gen. 12:2, 3). From the time of this call and promise, the story of Abraham belongs to the world.

Believing God and following that promise, he walked by faith alone, until the glow of that sublime trust became a beacon for the spiritual life of our race.

Abraham is possibly the most outstanding character in the world's religious history, outside of Christ. God promised to make his name great, and three mighty religions claim him in the line of their succession. Judaism looks back to him as the founder of the Hebrew nation, and the man who gave them their concept of the unity and spirituality of God. Moslems claim him by racial descent through Ishmael, and write his name on the roster of their mighty prophets. Christianity enrolls him among its heroes, and regards him as the progenitor of all those who walk by faith and not by sight. The foremost writer and theologian of Christendom said of him, "And if ye be Christ's, then are ye Abraham's seed, and heirs according to the promise" (Gal. 3:29). Therefore, Abraham looms as a gigantic figure on the horizon of history, and the way which he marked out remains clear after the lapse of four millenniums.

The fulfillment of the God-given promises was long delayed. The story of his life as told in Genesis is one of weary waiting and long-deferred hope. He was called into a country which God had given him and his offspring, yet he wandered over it as a stranger, living in tents, while other men tilled its soil and built its cities. All that he ever possessed of that land was a sepulchre where his bones might be laid. He was promised countless descendants, and yet the frosts of a century fell upon his childless head. He believed God when there was no prospect that he or his heirs would ever own that land, and "he staggered not at the promise of God through unbelief," when nature cried out that such a promise would never be fulfilled.

The Test of Faith

To understand the faith of Abraham, we must know the story as it is told in the Bible. We must see him waiting through tiresome years, amid the shadows, for the light which did not come, and for some tangible evidence which human expectation demanded. We must see him when the time seemed long and there was no visible manifestation, staying his heart upon God's bare promise, as he held to his unfaltering course.

The birth of the child of promise came at last, and the heart of Abraham must have been thrilled as he looked upon the long-expected heir. But just when faith seemed honored by promises fulfilled, the supreme test of his life came. Isaac was budding into young manhood, hope had blossomed into joyous confidence, and life to Abraham seemed full and complete. It was at this time that God made His supreme demand upon the faith of His loyal follower. He called upon Abraham to lay upon the prepared altar the child of his love and offer him to God in bloody sacrifice. He was asked to disannul the promises and destroy the full fruition of hope's expectation.

But even in that crucial hour, his faith in God won the victory, and he obeyed with a broken heart, still trusting in the immutability of the divine covenant. Even God could go no further with Abraham; there was no more trying ordeal through which he could pass. He now stood upon the loftiest pinnacle which human trust has yet climbed, and here is revealed the reach of his sublime faith and the spiritual grandeur of the man.

The story of how God prepared another sacrifice and His encomium upon Abraham is beautifully told in the holy record. No wonder he is called the father of the faithful.

To understand the glory of his victory, we must see the man in his environment. There was no long roll of heroes who had walked that way before him, in whose steps he might follow. There was no fellowship of saints to refresh his soul, when the way was tiresome and his heart was weary from waiting. Alone, without helper or companion, he made his lonely pilgrimage and fought his battles. There was no human helper, when he endured the soul-bruising test beside that altar of stone on Mount Moriah.

Shall we wonder that he was God's man to establish a new line and usher in a new day? They utterly fail to see his place in the eternal plans, who look upon him simply as the founder of a nation. His work was incomparably beyond that. He was a pioneer in comprehension of the nature and unity of God. One God—holy, eternal, spiritual and invisible —and that God made known to men through faith alone: this is the creed and majesty of Abraham. The world about him believed in countless deities and made images like unto themselves, but Abraham worshiped the unseen Jehovah.

Abraham Learned to Know God

No attempted likenesses of Jehovah adorned the altar where Abraham worshiped. Jehovah was to be known spiritually and through faith alone. Abraham taught the world that a believing heart rather than a knowing head is the right way of apprehending the most High. He was wise enough to understand that God is beyond the measure of human knowledge; that He can do things which human wisdom cannot fathom; and that there are promises which seem impossible to mortal minds and which bewilder unbelieving men. That which made other men doubt and fear did not trouble him in the least. He had the faith to understand farther than he could see, and his concept of God made the incredible the joyful anticipation of his hope. Faith after the order of Abraham's looks at the promises of the eternal God, and not at the circumstances; and does not despair when His promises are beyond man's comprehension. It beholds Him who is invisible and places no interrogation points in His covenants.

The contribution of Abraham to the Christian faith lies in his conception of the unity and holiness of Jehovah, and that God made known through faith. Having the knowledge that comes by faith, he trampled impossibilities under his feet. He gave testimony that men can know God through the simple experience of obedient faith, and this testimony became the ground of his greatness. Such faith seems foolish to the worldly-wise, but it is the sanest philosophy and, at the same time, the most potent force among men.

Faith in some truth or cause has been the mainspring of every mighty life. It has made possible the lasting renown of men like Moses, David, Paul, Carey, Müeller and Moody. The faith of Abraham was in God, His faithfulness and the steadfastness of His word. He believed God without wavering and pressed on in his God-appointed way until the years of manhood's strength had passed into history.

This solitary pilgrim was known as the friend of God. Other men might make human contacts and form earthly alliances, but Abraham lived on terms of intimacy with the most High. Not many among the great of earth sought his friendship, but the God who numbered the stars and calleth them by their names came in human form to sit with him under the old oak at Mamre. He was a man whom God could trust. When the doom of death was hanging over the foul cities of the plain, God said: "Shall I hide from Abraham that thing which I do? . . . For I know him, that he will command his children and his household after him, and they shall keep the way of the LORD" (Gen. 18:17, 19). No loftier honor can come to mortal man than to be a confidant of the Almighty.

Out of Weakness Made Strong

Abraham was not faultless, as the record plainly tells us. No man is great along every line, and this man had his human weaknesses. His cowardly falsehoods about Sarah and his treatment of Hagar are blots upon the escutcheon of his greatness. They remind us that he was a man with the infirmities of our common clay. However, these things should not blind us to the real bigness of the man. It is true of the holiest among the saints, that they like the weakest of us have "this treasure in earthen vessels." Let us behold the mighty faith that lifted him to a lofty place in the drama of redemption, and made him an explorer of the way for all men to follow, if they would know God.

Abraham built no city, but all his life he sought for one "which hath foundations, whose builder and maker is God"; and his example has inspired myriads in that same ly quest. He possessed no earthly country, but desired a "bett country, that is, an heavenly," and led the life of a nomad in the land which God had promised him.

Abraham was not brilliant; he penned no words of wisdom which the ages have cherished. He was not a statesman, and only once did he show a flash of military genius. As a wandering chieftain, following a dream at which the unbelieving sneered, he wrote his name among the immortals. He wrote no word of his sublime creed, yet a thousand pens have tried to tell the story of his living faith. He composed no songs, yet a myriad of poetic souls have striven to sing the

Iliad of his long trek and its patient vigils. His only sanctuary was a rude altar of stone, but uncounted temples and cathedrals are now standing because of the faith which he showed to men.

Abraham believed God and because of his faith he became a stranger and a pilgrim in the earth. Believing the promise of God, he looked through the long years to its fruition, and some day the world will rejoice in the glory of its actual fulfillment. Believing God, he bound the son whom God had given him, laid him upon the altar, and lifted the knife to spill his blood. This final and supreme test brought from Jehovah the encomium, "Now I know that thou fearest God, seeing thou hast not withheld thy son, thine only son from me." God kept His word to this exile of faith, and multitudes who know not the name of any world-ruler of Abraham's day are inspired and thrilled by this epic of his life. He believed God, and millions have followed him out of the shadows into the light.

In the splendor of his faith, Abraham stands before us greater than any sage or ruler of Egypt or Chaldea, and exerts a thousand times more influence on the present generation. No wearer of imperial purple, no marshal of conquering legions has so stirred the hearts of men to holy endeavor, or so taught them to endure hardness and wait for the unfolding of the eternal plans, as Abraham.

He died full of years, satisfied with life, and went to be with Him whom he followed so long in the darkness. From that city that hath foundations, God's pioneer of the faithful watches the fulfillment of that divine promise, the full glory of which will be realized when the host who have emulated his faith meet their spiritual father in that land where murky shades no longer make dim the exceeding great and precious promises of God.

"He knew not the path where he wandered:
  He knew not the journey before,
As the days of his pilgrimage lengthened,
  And life to its eventide wore;
And oft by his tent in the desert
  He dreamed of the way he had trod,
Ere he sought for the beautiful city
  Whose builder and maker is God.

"Above were the stars for his compass,
  Beneath him the Syrian sands,
And only a promise to lead him
  Through dreary and desolate lands;
Who doubts his faith must have wavered,
  As he wandered with weariness shod,
In quest of the glorified city
  Whose builder and maker is God?

"He lay by his tent in the even,
  And o'er him night's pageantry rolled;
The stars in their crystalline orbits,
  The moon down a highway of gold;
And ever he heard it, the whisper,
  Press onward o'er pathways untrod;
There waits you the wonderful city
  Whose builder and maker is God.

"He was broken and aged and weary,
  He longed for the city of rest;
And doubt stood beside him to question,
  'Is the way you have chosen the best?'
Yet still he pressed onward and forward,
  O'er sand of the desert and clod,

Still seeking the peace of the city
    Whose builder and maker is God.

"One night the great stars in their courses
    Blazed o'er him and glittered and burned,
As he sank by the side of a brooklet,
    And his soul for its heritage yearned.
'I am weary,' he murmured; 'no longer
    May I on my pilgrimage plod;
Yet grant me one glimpse of the city
    Whose builder and maker is God.'

"They found him at daybreak; the breezes
    Above him a requiem sung;
One cloud and its shadow crept eastward
    And o'er him a cerement flung;
Yet he smiled as a sleeper who dreameth
    Of fields that the angels have trod,
And they knew that he looked on the city
    Whose builder and maker is God."

References: Genesis, chapters 11 to 26; John 8:39–58; Acts 7:2–32; Galatians 3:6–18, 29; Hebrews 7:1–9.

Job

THE MAN UPON WHOM THE DEVIL
WAS TURNED LOOSE

G OD was proud of Job. He boasted of him to the devil. He
delighted in his sincerity and unselfish devotion. He
looked down into the heart of Job and found no alloy in the
gold of his loving service. When Satan, after journeying
over the earth, came into the presence of God, he was asked if
he had seen Job.

Now Job was the best man in the world, and in God's sight
the most important thing in the world. In fact, the biggest
thing in the world is a real man, and the best thing in the
world is a good man. The most attractive thing in the world
is a beautiful character. Moral beauty is much fairer to those
who can appreciate it than any sort of physical beauty. Man
is bigger than a mountain, an ocean, or a continent; and
goodness is fairer than a flower, a rainbow, or a brilliant sun-
set. In the sight of God, Job was the most prominent and
attractive thing upon the earth; and so He asked Satan if he
had considered Job.

At once the devil showed just how devilish he is; listen to
his answer: "Doth Job fear God for nought? Hast not thou
made an hedge about him, and about his house, and about all
that he hath on every side? Thou hast blessed the work of
his hands, and his substance is increased in the land. But put
forth thine hand now, and touch all that he hath, and he will
curse thee to thy face" (Job 1:9–11).

Now the devil really thought that he was telling the truth.

Evil cannot understand goodness, and being utterly selfish Satan could not appreciate genuine, loving service. He believed that every man could be bought, and that all human conduct is built upon selfishness. His followers are like him. The men who cry that every man has his price, and that no woman is pure, are just like their father, unable to apprehend true honesty and essential purity. All that they prove when they echo this age-long lie is that they are for sale themselves, and that their lives are rotten.

God accepted the challenge of the devil. He knew that Job was sincere in his service, and that the devil could not break the bond between Him and a good man, upheld by His abounding grace. God affirmed that a good man with an abiding faith in Him was more than a match for the devil. Job knew nothing of all this, and God did not intend that he should. He told Satan to do his worst, but to keep his hands off of Job's person. The slanderer had said that Job was serving God for what he could get, and so God allowed him to deal with the possessions and family of Job, and see what he could do.

The Devices of the Devil

At once Satan did his best—which was at the same time his worst. In one day all the property of Job was swept away, and all his children died in one dreadful catastrophe. The man who arose in the morning the richest and most envied man in all the East, who looked into the faces of manly sons and fair daughters, sat down in the shadows of evening a childless pauper. The devil chuckled and waited; he really believed that Job would fall. Listen, however, to God's hero! He looked at his empty fields, gazed into the cold faces of his children, bowed his head and cried, "Naked came I out of my mother's womb, and naked shall I return thither: the

where Job was, other folk cannot help him very much; he must have something deep down inside to sustain him. No merely ethical code or sickly sentimentality will suffice; one must really lay hold upon God by faith and live that way. It takes more than some pretty theories about God to give joy to a sick pauper on an ash heap!

Job was completely staggered and discouraged, and like many another under like conditions he wanted to die. Though he longed for death, he would not surrender his trust in Jehovah. Satan had done his worst, and coldly waited to rejoice in the collapse of Job and the disappointment of Jehovah.

The good man was terribly bewildered by that which had befallen him. He looked for God who seemed to hide Himself, and all of Job's ideas about life had gone awry. He knew that his heart had been honest in the service of Jehovah, yet things were terribly out of joint. His property and children had been taken; his health and comfort of body were now gone; his mind was confused and his heart was broken. He cried out for death! The future looked bleak and hopeless, and he saw nothing worth while before him. God was swathed in thick clouds and darkness, and Job for a while felt himself forsaken of heaven and misunderstood upon earth. He turned every way seeking some light and surcease of sorrow; life was empty and death would not come. There was no consolation in the words of his friends; they only added to his pain, and in his own experiences he found no explanation for what had come upon him.

The Victory of Faith

Here we come to the greatness and victory of Job. Turning from the admonitions of friends who only darkened counsel with a multitude of words, and forgetting for an instant his

own sorrows and his bruised and bleeding heart, he stead-
fastly exercised his faith in God and cried, "Though he slay
me, yet will I trust in him" (Job 13:15). Here we find the
supreme lesson in the career of Job:—God's true child trusts
Him when he does not know, and holds on by faith when he
cannot see.

There is a message in Isaiah which was given for times
like those through which Job passed. It was written for those
who do not have the strength which Job had—for his trials
were before the day of Isaiah. It reads like this: "Who is
among you that feareth the LORD, that obeyeth the voice of
his servant, that walketh in darkness, and hath no light? let
him trust in the name of the LORD, and stay upon his God"
(Isa. 50:10). This is the way that Job did when the clouds
were thickest and all the stars were hidden; and the man or
woman who can do this will not walk alone, for God in His
own way and in His own time will reveal Himself.

Satan heard this word of Job and slunk away, and we hear
no more of him in the story. He knew that he was beaten,
for no man who thus speaks in such an hour can ever fail.
Satan did his utmost to destroy Job, but was ignominiously
defeated. The man sitting in the dust trusted God when
he could not understand.

Job stands before the world as an example of what may be
achieved by every trusting child of God. He had been robbed
of all earthly sources of happiness, and when everything before his eyes cried out that God had deserted him, he kept on
believing and walked out where there seemed to be no path
for his feet. There is no such thing as crushing men like
Job. They look at the unseen and step out in the impenetrable
darkness to find themselves led by the light of infinite love.

There are many of God's children who walk in shrouded
paths with broken hearts and bleeding feet. They eat the

ashen crust of sorrow, moistened with their tears. They wait through sleepless nights for the light that does not come. So God put in His Book the story of this good man on whom the devil was turned loose, that men may learn the secret of his victory, and remember that God watches over His own with tender love and infinite compassion, while they pass through the refining furnace.

The Devil Was Defeated

Job's hour of victory came. The sorrow which endured through the long night was followed by the morning of light and triumph, and up from that ash heap of pain rose the loftiest note of the Old Testament:—"For I know that my redeemer liveth, and that he shall stand at the latter day upon the earth: and though after my skin worms destroy this body, yet in my flesh shall I see God: whom I shall see for myself, and mine eyes shall behold, and not another; though my reins be consumed within me" (Job 19:25–27). It was worth all the loneliness, sorrow and poverty to give the world a word like that. If Job had said nothing else, that sentence alone would lift him among the stars.

The devil was defeated and Job was victorious, though the man was not conscious of the greatness of his triumph. He did not look much like a conqueror, covered with boils and sitting in the ashes; but victories like that are often gained in just such places. God was looking on and knew the glory of that overcoming. He put the story in His imperishable Record that it might help other children who walk along like roads.

There was no blare of trumpets or streaming banners about that battleground, but the heavenly host rejoiced and sang hosannas which will not be forgotten. Battles of this sort are fought on the inside, where men live; and the struggle

is never lost, unless the man fails in his inner self; but Job
did not fail. Job defeated the devil on his own battlefield,
and God placed his name on the honor roll, and will put
beside it the name of any one, however humble, who wins a
fight like that.

"Long years ago as earth lay dark and still,
There rose a cry upon a lonely hill;
While in the frailty of our human clay
Christ our Redeemer passed the self-same way.

"Still stands His cross from that dread hour to this,
Like some bright star above the dark abyss;
Still through the veil the Victor's pitying eyes
Look down to bless our lesser Calvaries."

References: Job, entire book; Ezekiel 14:12–20; James 5:11.

Esau

THE MAN WHO COULD NOT WAIT

A PAIR of twins is always interesting. Some twins are just alike and afford endless diversion for friends and neighbors, as they try to distinguish one from the other. Yet twins are interesting when they are utterly unlike. The pair that came to Isaac and Rebekah were just about as different as it was possible for two babies to be. You would never have guessed from their appearance that they were even remotely related. One of them was ruddy of face and grew up into a burly, bearded man with red, hairy hands and arms; the other was pale and quiet with smooth, hairless body and hands like a woman. One could hardly think of brothers more unlike than these two. They were just as different in mind and habits as in body. Esau was full of animal spirits, a fellow who loved the field and the chase; while Jacob was quiet, industrious and home loving.

Esau usually made the best first impression, and was the favorite of casual observers. He was a sturdy, fresh-looking, high-colored youngster who threw himself with hearty zest into everything. He looked much stronger and more vigorous than his retiring, pale-faced brother. However, those who observed closely learned that Esau always played the best game at the beginning, and was soon ready to quit, but that Jacob often won the victory because he did not seem to know how to quit.

Esau was certainly a fine-looking fellow as he strode out in the morning with bow in hand and his quiver of arrows thrown over his shoulder. No wonder that the quiet Isaac gloried in the lusty manhood of his first-born; he was just the opposite of all that his father had been. I am sure that most of the neighbors said, "What a pity that Jacob is not a strong, fine-looking fellow like Esau."

As they grew older, the difference became more apparent: Esau spent his days in the fields and forest, delighting in the chase, while the staid Jacob remained at home helping his mother and day-dreaming about the future. The mother soon learned that when a task called for time and patience, it should be given to Jacob. He did most of the drudgery, while Esau was hunting and having a good time with the fellows of his sort. Jacob did not care for hunting, it looked like a waste of time; and Jacob had some big ideas in that head of his.

Jacob Learned to Wait

Jacob did not have a very high quality of moral standards, but he knew that nothing worth while ever came without working and waiting, and he was willing to wait. Right here is where Esau failed; he had no long look upon life; he did not learn that the best things of life do not fall into the laps of those who are always in a hurry. The privileges of the first-born belonged to him, but they meant little because their possession was in the faraway future, and he wanted his good things right now. A birthright that would not come to him until the death of Isaac did not mean much to Esau; yet the future blessings and advantages of that birthright were keeping Jacob awake at nights. He wanted the covenant blessings and reasoned that as Esau did not care for those things he had just as well have them.

Jacob is by no means to be justified in the way he went about getting the birthright, but he appreciated the value of it and Esau did not, and Jacob knew the weakness of Esau. The Bible story is short and there is far more than appears on the surface of the record. If we will think a bit, we can see Esau—careless, ease-loving—seeking present pleasure and gratification, while Jacob is looking anxiously down the years and biding his time.

Esau came in from hunting one day empty-handed, tired and hungry. Jacob had been looking for just such an occasion, and he had everything ready. When Esau came in, Jacob was stirring some red pottage in a pot. He had prepared that pottage with great care; he had cooked it for Esau and it was going to be the most expensive dish that Esau had ever eaten. How good it smelled! Esau cried, "Jacob, give me some of that pottage; I'm starving to death!" Now Jacob knew that was not exactly true, but it was no time to argue with Esau. I do not think that Jacob answered at first; he just kept stirring the pot and letting the tent fill with the savory odor of the food. "Please give me something to eat; I'm going to die if I don't get some food. You have no idea how hungry I am; I chased an old deer all day and could not get within bow shot of it. You surely won't let me die just for the lack of a little pottage!"

Now that was the time for which Jacob had been looking, and he began to bargain a little. "What will you give me for it, brother?" Jacob waited a little before he continued. He lifted the lid of the vessel, while the nostrils of Esau twitched and his mouth fairly watered. "Will you sell me your birthright?" asked Jacob, looking meanwhile into the fire.

Esau caught his breath; this was more than he had considered; but what did the old birthright mean? He was going to die if he did not get that pottage, and what good would the birthright do a dead man. A full stomach meant more to him at that moment than a fortune in the distant future. Yet he did not answer right away, and Jacob lifted the cover and stirred the red pottage again. "All right," said Esau. "But hurry! I am awfully hungry!"

Jacob did not hurry; he meant to have that birthright, and there was no need of making any mistake. He appreciated to the full what it meant, but poor Esau did not and, worst of all, could not. The very deliberation of Jacob only fired the impatience of Esau and made him more intensely eager. Jacob repeated the formula of a binding contract and asked Esau to swear to it.

It may be that Esau hesitated a moment at this point, but the breeze coming through the tent brought to his nose the aroma of the pot, and the die was cast. After the manner of the times, he repeated the solemn oath that sealed the agreement, while Jacob smiled to himself and poured the pottage into an earthen dish. How good that pottage tasted! How Esau guzzled it down and smacked his lips! In a little while the meal was over, and Esau swaggered out, a full-fed animal, but with no birthright.

The Saddest Word—It Might Have Been

Of course, the time would come when Esau would want the birthright very badly, but that did not trouble him then, and like an animal whose appetite is sated he stalked away. Esau had been in no danger of dying—strong men do not die from hunger that easily. The trouble was that Esau was not willing to wait. Waiting is one of the finest arts this world knows anything about. Waiting is something unknown to animal appetites, and calls for qualities to which the flesh is a stranger. Patience is a human trait, and the word belongs to the vocabulary of the rational and spiritual. Esau was a representative of those who live to the flesh. The body clamors for the gratification of its desires immediately, and knows no time save the present.

Some folk wonder why God chose Jacob; well, I do not know as much about the secrets of predestination as some people seem to know, but when we understand the stuff of which men are made, the reason, in part at least, is not hard to find. Many of God's promises are for the future; the best things do not belong to the here and now. Objects of the rarest worth come to men as the result of patient toil and steadfast devotion to some lofty objective. The man who has the far look, who peers through the telescope of faith and hope, is the man for whom God is looking. All the Esaus in the world never builded a city, never wrote a book, never painted a great picture, never lifted the world one inch nearer God. The worth-while things are done by those who know how to toil through long and seemingly fruitless days, who mix their mortar with sweat, and mingle tears with their bread as they wait.

The wasted lives of earth are the Esau lives, the lives of those who want all they are going to get right now. In this manner of life we see the germ of a long list of crimes that have blighted the earth. What is theft but the act of the fellow who cannot wait? He knows that real gain comes as the reward of labor and patience, but he is in a hurry and cannot wait. All crooked and fraudulent business is born of the same ancestry. It cries, "I cannot wait; I am at the point of death." So the birthright of honor is bartered for the red pottage of the quick return.

Poor Esau! The time came when he wanted that birthright very much, when he sought "it earnestly with tears," but the man who cannot wait and will not wait must wait, and will wait forever for the things which he has lost. The picture of Esau as he went out disappointed from the presence of blind Isaac is that of every man who traffics the birthright of better things in the future for the gratification of the moment.

In one of the finest portraits that a master artist ever drew, old John Bunyan pictures that company: "I saw moreover in my dream that the Interpreter took him by the hand, and led him into a little room, where sat two children, each one in his chair. The name of the eldest was Passion, and the name of the other Patience. Passion seemed to be much discontented, but Patience was very quiet. . . . Then I saw one come to Passion, and brought him a bag of treasure, and poured it down at his feet; the which he took up and rejoiced therein, and withal laughed Patience to scorn. But I beheld but a while, and he had lavished all away, and had nothing left him but rags." Old John knew a lot about human nature and how the battle of life is won. The Esaus trade the future for the treasure-bag of present gratification and have only rags at the end.

The Folly of Not Waiting

Poor Benedict Arnold was a member of the Esau family. He was brilliant, brave and beloved by the soldiers, but he could not wait. The struggle for liberty was too long; the honors he craved seemed too far away, and the rewards of patriotism did not travel fast enough; so he sold the birthright of honor and loyalty for the sodden pottage of British gold, and won only the scorn of those who had bought him.

The clan of Esau is one of the largest in all the world, but possibly the most noted of all of them is Judas Iscariot who sold his Lord, and sent his name down the centuries as a synonym for all that is false in faith and treacherous in friendship. Many of this company do not mean to be wicked and waste all that is worth-while, but they just will not wait! The defaulters who have used the other fellow's money because they were in a hurry to get rich belong to the Esau family. The bright boys who started well, and then through the love of ease and the lure of the flesh have failed to realize life's heavenly vision, have fallen just as Esau fell.

Esau is one of the pitiable characters of the old Book: not big enough to make a tragedy, but just a poor, miserable failure, for the simple reason that he could not endure the loss of the red pottage of the present and tarry for better things. Mark Antony might have gone down in history in the place of Augustus, if he had ever learned this lesson. Poor fellow! He could not say to the call of the lusty flesh, "You must wait; honor and the empire are first." The smiles and embraces of Cleopatra belonged to the present, and "drunk with her caresses," he "madly threw a world away."

Waiting is not an easy task! Sometimes the hardest thing in the world is just to wait—wait for the right time, the fitting time, for God's time. It was in this that the force of our Lord's temptation lay. He was tempted to win the things for which He came without the long and bitter struggle. He was offered the short and easy way, a way that had no Gethsemane with its hours of awful agony, that had no Calvary with its cross and the lonely darkness. He was offered the kingdoms of the world without the age-long struggle through which He has waited to see the "travail of His soul."

The Wisdom of Waiting

Yes, waiting is manful work, and the Esaus are not the strong men of the earth. Not very many are big enough to wait, while the other fellow who goes the short, easy way seems to slip in so easily. To have some things just within our grasp and turn our backs upon them because of the greater value of that which comes with the long years of waiting is many times very, very hard.

Our Lord is the master waiter of all time. He met and overcame all the temptations that come to the Esaus. The devil told Him that with just a little compromise, just a little stoop, there would be no need for the agony of the bloody sweat; but Jesus was willing to wait. He chose the long way, the slow way, the hard way, and He is still waiting. The kingdom is coming, very slowly it seems, but He is waiting; and the glory of a many-diademed victory will come to the One who is "expecting till his enemies be made his footstool."

The Esaus start well and seem to be getting the best; in fact, it looks sometimes as if they were getting all that is best. They dazzle us with their lusty strength and embarrass us with the trophies of their skill; yet they miss the best of life, and the rarest treasures and greatest victories are not for them, because they cannot wait.

Think of the waiting and working of Adoniram Judson in Burma! Seven years had slipped away and not one convert for all those days of toil.

"How is it, Judson?"

"Bright as the promises of God."

There is a waiter for you—one who could work and wait and sing the while.

"Morrison, what are you doing? They will never let you into China."

"Oh, I am translating the Bible into Chinese; somebody will get in someday and will need what I am doing."

The years have flown, and Burma is dotted with Christian churches, and China is honeycombed with Christian institutions; all because these men of God knew how to wait. The Esaus are the yoke-wearers of the world; they will always have to serve the Jacobs. The real rewards and the true victories

come to those who have learned in the truest sense the royal
lesson of waiting.

"Be strong!
We are not here to play, to dream, to drift;
We have hard work to do, and loads to lift;
Shun not the struggle—face it; 'tis God's gift.

"Be strong!
Say not, 'The days are evil. Who's to blame?'
And fold the hands and acquiesce—oh shame!
Stand up, speak out, and bravely, in God's name.

"Be strong!
It matters not how deep intrenched the wrong,
How hard the battle goes, the day how long;
Faint not—fight on! Tomorrow comes the song."

References: Genesis, chapters 25 to 33; Malachi 1:2, 3; Hebrews 11:20; 12:16.

Jochebed

A MIGHTY MOTHER

To HAVE a great mother is the first steppingstone toward great distinction. God's first contribution to the towering achievements of Moses was Jochebed. We know little of the father of Moses. Amram had little claim to fame apart from his illustrious son, for Jochebed had more to do with the making of his life. It was no easy matter for a woman to make herself felt in the days in which she lived, but human nature has not changed in all these millenniums. Whenever a woman is stronger and more intelligent than her husband, he will be second lieutenant in the family, whether they live in the full blaze of the twentieth century or in the year 1600 B.C.

Jochebed lived and died a slave; it is doubtful if she ever drew a breath of freedom. Yet this poor bondwoman left her impress upon all time. We know little of her early life; she was born a slave of slave parents into a life of slavery; all her relatives were slaves. Slavery, however, in that day did not mean inferiority of blood or character; the fortunes of war often made the rulers of one generation serfs in the next. This woman was of the line of Abraham, and had the shrewdness of Rebecca without her deception.

Her famous son was born just at the time when Pharaoh had determined to stop the rapid increase of the Hebrews by destroying all the newly-born male children. It was a foolish thing upon the part of the great monarch, for he thus challenged the purposes of Jehovah and the biggest force in human nature, that mighty dynamic of mother-love.

Despite the edict of the monarch, this poor slave-mother resolved that her baby should not die. For three months, she kept him hidden in the home; and when the healthy-growing youngster could no longer be concealed, she called all her God-given wisdom into play to save his life. It was Pharaoh against Jochebed—all the power of Egypt against one poor slave-mother. It did not look like a fair contest; that mighty monarch had said that her baby must die, while that mother had vowed that he should live. Of course, all along there was the overruling providence of God; but when God wants to do big things, He picks tested and yielded tools.

Jochebed hid her baby with great care until the time came when it was impossible to conceal him longer. He was growing and his lusty cries were getting louder every day. How she must have lain in the darkness with her little one hugged to her breast, dreading the coming of some Egyptian officer who would hurl him into the Nile! Something must be done! The inquisitors were becoming more stringent in enforcing the law and more thorough in their search. How she shuddered as her baby boy cried when some of the cruel spies were passing by! Necessity was upon Jochebed; some would have said it was impossible to do more, but this mother was one of those who achieved the insuperable.

The Venture of Faith

How she dreamed and planned and prayed, until at last a desperate expedient was born of the love and genius of that heroic soul! Jochebed knew the superstitions of the Egyptians about the mighty Nile—so different from all the other rivers —and finally she determined to risk her baby with the crocodiles of the great river rather than the cruelty of Pharaoh. The ruler of Egypt had conquered mighty nations, but he had never encountered a courage and resourcefulness like that of this Hebrew mother. Her brave heart and keen brain planned that her boy should live, and her plans were shaped by wisdom born of a mighty faith in God and an unconquerable love.

She wove a little ark of the bulrushes that grew by the river brink and made it waterproof with pitch. Never in all time was such a craft destined to bear such priceless freight. Not the fabled Argos of Jason with the golden fleece carried a treasure comparable to this. Imagine that scene, as she went down to the river ere morning had dawned. Jochebed bore in her arms the treasured babe, while little Miriam trudged along with that tiny ark whose cargo would change the tale of history. The place chosen was near the favorite bathing place of the wealthy Egyptian women, where there would be comparative safety from the reptiles of the stream. Some might say that the coming of the royal lady to that particular spot was only accidental, but we may be sure that Jochebed knew all about the place where she was placing her baby; faith does not preclude common sense.

How carefully she placed her precious boy in the little boat, and tucked about him such simple covering as her poverty was able to furnish! One last kiss and a smothered sob, and she turned away to pray and wait. How long it seemed! How the mother heart ached while hopes rose and fell! Miriam, with the usual privilege of an elder sister, waited nearby. How her breast throbbed, as she watched that richly-dressed company coming down to the river! The time seemed long as the women sported in the warm tide. Would nothing ever happen?

Suddenly the women heard a tiny cry. "What is that? Sounds like a baby!" Again they heard it, and someone spied the little ship with its unusual freight. A swimmer went out and brought it in. "Look! a baby! What is a baby doing in such a place?"

The princess knew what had happened; some poor Israelitish woman, despairing of keeping her child, had resolved to trust the river and its saurians rather than the heartless king. As they turned back the simple covers from the little face, a pitiful wail of hunger went up, and the baby lips puckered in the only language which he knew, the oldest and most universal in the world. The heart of the childless woman beat a little quicker. What would she not give for a child like that? Look at those rounded cheeks! Those lips were like tiny rose buds! That ear curled like a sea shell! Those wonderful dark eyes awaken love in her heart! Once more that heart-clinging baby cry and her decision was made; this babe should live! She would keep him and tell Pharaoh that he was the gift of the sacred river, and that would make him safe. The first round of the fight between Pharaoh and the poor slave-mother was over, and the referee marked it down for Jochebed; her boy was safe. The monarch of Egypt never dreamed how badly he was beaten!

As the company went back, tenderly bearing the babe along, a small, ragged, Hebrew girl bowed before them. How diplomatic she was! "The great lady has taken the baby from the river, but will she not need a nurse for him?" She tells the princess that she knows a woman of her people who would make a wonderful nurse. Shrewd little Miriam! Or had Jochebed already thought of all that as she planned her struggle on bended knee? Hurrah for Jochebed! She has saved her boy, and she has maneuvered Pharaoh into paying her for doing that which she would have given her all to have the chance of doing. Another round is over, and again the judges give the decision to the slave-mother. Was there ever just such a contest? The son of Jochebed lived and the king who had doomed him to death was paying his mother to nurse him! *The Test of Faith*

The Triumph of Faith

There were wise men in Egypt in those days; right learned and clever were the priests of her temples; sage in lore were the counsellors of the monarch of the double crown, but I make bold to say that the wisest head and bravest heart in all that wondrous land was that of this brave slave-mother. She had outwitted them all and won so completely that her boy was trained in all the learning of the scholars and philosophers in that land. Providence? Yes, to be sure, but none the less a triumph for the mother who planned and worked while she prayed and trusted.

Jochebed bore her son in her arms during the days of his childhood, and his first lessons came from her lips. The lords of Egypt still reveled and the people of Jochebed toiled to build the treasure houses of their tyrant, but during those stressful days Jochebed fought the fight of faith, and won the final battle of that memorable struggle.

Jochebed was a child of the covenants; her faith was in the unseen Jehovah of her fathers. All about her was the revolting idolatry of Egypt, with its gorgeous temples and imposing worship; and well she knew that its philosophy and religion would seek to claim the mind and heart of her son. Again she waged battle, this time for the soul of the son of her love. With a vision that looked beyond the fleeting present, she poured into his plastic soul the promises of the God of Abraham and the hopes of Israel.

As she had loved the unconscious babe and wrestled against unreckonable odds for the preservation of his life, so with even more meaningful love and wiser planning she set herself to keep him for the God of the covenants. The fact that her son might fill the throne of world empire and wear the double crown of the valley of the Nile were as nothing in comparison with the oracles of her God and the faith of her fathers. Truly it might have been said of her before it was of Moses, "She endured as seeing him that was invisible."

The battle was on, Jochebed versus Egypt. It was now a bigger fight than ever against overpowering odds. Yet the faith of this mother did not falter, and the courage of her heart did not fail. On the one side were mighty schools and mitered priests, with all the glamor of wealth and the trappings of royalty; on the other was a poor slave-mother in her humble home of poverty. Her hope and her faith were in the God who had called Abraham and guided Joseph. The odds were not so great as it seemed to those who did not know Jochebed and her God, for she had enlisted the unseen power of the great I AM.

Great Mothers Have Great Faith

In the midst of darkness, her faith leaped the barriers of poverty and serfdom, and over the intervening years caught a glimpse of the coming glory. She was in line with the eternal plans, and on her knees, pleading the promises made to her fathers, she was mightier than all the legions that marched at the feet of Pharaoh. Jochebed, pouring into the heart of her boy the faith that made Abraham a wanderer and Jacob an exile, was a more potent force than all the proud priests in the temples of Thebes or the columned sanctuaries of Karnak. There was no possibility of conquering a faith and love like hers. It cried, "Pharaoh, you shall not kill my boy; Egypt, you shall not destroy the soul of my son"; that was Jochebed's declaration of war, and right valiantly did she keep her word.

The world may not know it, but back of the life of nearly

every great man is an unusual mother. There is no earthly love like hers; it enfolds the babe ere consciousness has dawned; it guards the helpless days of childhood; it shields that life with prayers, and hallows it with sacred memories. The world may disown and reject her boy; it may even destroy him; yet mother love will find him in the gutter and gather the soiled, unkempt form to her bosom, and whisper words of faith and hope. He may wear the disgrace of the condemned felon, but mother love will stand with bleeding soul beneath the shadow of the gibbet, take the lifeless form when men are done with it, bedew it with tears, and sob out its life over the neglected grave. Kipling tells this story in his beautiful little poem, "Mother o' Mine."

> "If I were hung on the highest hill,
>   Mother o' mine, O mother o' mine;
> I know whose love would follow me still,
>   Mother o' mine, O mother o' mine.

> "If I were drowned in the deepest sea,
>   Mother o' mine, O mother o' mine;
> I know whose tears would come down to me,
>   Mother o' mine, O mother o' mine."

Moses was ready, when the time came, for a choice which would alter the currents of the ages. His sublime decision has been glorified in both human and divine records. Where did Moses learn the knowledge of the true God and the fear of Jehovah that made him spurn a crown and cast his lot with the serfdom of Israel? Who told him of "the recompense of reward" which would follow the "reproach of Christ" for whom he suffered? May we not believe that during those fateful years that devoted mother poured into his opening mind the stories of his people and the covenants of Jehovah?

What a vision that mother had! Thrones could not dazzle her, and palaces could not dim her sense of holy values. Her faith was not for sale, though the world offered the highest price in the purse of its power. She dreamed of something better for the child she had borne than to wear the diadem of earth's proudest throne and reign over the valley of the Nile. Here was a mother who could look beyond the majesty of thrones and the glamour of palaces, and see the glory of the on-moving purposes of God. God needed a man, but the baby must be before the man, and the mother before the babe. The ark of the bulrushes must precede the ark of the covenant in the wilderness, and the foiling of the Pharaoh of the oppression before the humbling of the Pharaoh of the Exodus. Before Moses could appreciate the burning bush, he must learn to know the God of the smoking furnace of the Abrahamic covenant. Before he could stand upon the cloud-robed mount and receive from the hand of Jehovah the laws for the ages, he must hear from his mother's lips of the God who destroyed Sodom and wrestled with Jacob at Jabbok.

Yes, I repeat, it was Pharaoh against Jochebed, Osiris versus Jehovah; the priests of a thousand gilded shrines against the faith and prayers of one lonely slave-mother. The battle was won about that cradle on the knees of Jochebed. She won by faith and prayer and the courage of that mother love. When Moses turned from the treasures of Egypt and cast his lot with the enslaved sons of Jacob, it was a greater victory than that won by Alexander at Arbela, or when the Roman put his foot on the neck of the world. Hats off to this slave-mother! Egypt could not rob her of the son of her love, and all the stately and templed idolatry of the land of Rameses and Necho could not shake his faith which first dwelt in his mother's heart mid the poverty of bondage.

Moses is the monument of Jochebed. The plagues of Egypt were the fulfillment of her hopes. The divided sea and the laws which have buttressed civilizations are in part the trophies of her faith and love. God used her, it is true, but only such a woman of faith could be used in such an hour. Pharaoh could enslave the nation, but he could not conquer the soul and brain of that lone Hebrew mother. She thwarted his laws, outwitted his spies, and brought his wealth to feed and clothe her son, while she kept his mighty brain and dauntless soul and humble heart for Israel and the world.

References: Exodus 6:20; Numbers 26:59.

Aaron

ONE OF THE NEAR GREAT

IT IS an awkward thing to be the elder brother of a really great man. Older brothers, early in life, form the habit of looking down upon the younger members of the family. They feel strongly the sense of superiority which comes from larger size and longer experience. Even in mature years, they find it hard to realize that their younger brother may have as much sense as they have.

Aaron was, much of the time, a more popular man than Moses. He was a more fluent speaker, and no doubt possessed the affability and gracious manner of the accomplished orator. It is remarkable how little prominence is given to oratory in the Bible; there were not many orators mightily used of God. Honesty, sincerity and faithfulness were more highly prized than the ability to weave magic webs of words, paint wonderful pictures, and sway the hearts of men with the wizardry of the lips.

Moses was slow of speech; he could not always find words to express the big ideas which made his brain a very furnace of molten thought. His tongue cleaved to the roof of his mouth as he felt about for phrases to convey the import of his mighty concepts and far-reaching plans. When Moses took up his pen in some quiet place, he wrote words that will never die. He penned things so big, so grand and sublime, that men have been stopping to read them for nearly thirty-five hundred years, and still treasure them among the classics which make up the precious heritage of humanity.

Aaron could speak charmingly; he could take the blunt, terse words of Moses and just make them live to those downtrodden Hebrews. One should not wonder if both Pharaoh and Israel thought the eloquent Aaron the bigger man of the two. Moses was for a time in the background, while his golden-mouthed brother held the limelight. All through their experiences in Egypt, Aaron got along well; he was the spokesman, and doubtless felt the self-mesmerism which belongs to many great orators. There is no man more fully aware of his own importance than the master of words, who feels his listeners sway under the necromancy of his burning utterances. Of course, Aaron felt the spell of those memorable days when the hand of Jehovah was heavy upon the land of Mizraim; it could not have been otherwise. The wonder of those stupendous miracles, the storm, the darkness, the death of the firstborn, and the crossing of the Red Sea must have fascinated and mastered him.

The Danger of Popularity

We have said that Aaron was more popular than Moses; they were always together, and Aaron did most of the talking, taking the plain, simple words of his brother and making them sound good in the ears of the people. It would seem that his person was more attractive, according to the eastern standards of manly beauty. We read of the beard that reached his girdle; and when wearing the priestly vestments, he must have been a striking and commanding figure.

The rabble are slow to appreciate real worth; they seldom look below the surface of things; and for that reason it took Israel a long time to form a fitting estimate of Moses. But Aaron—they could see that flowing beard and hear the tones of that resonant voice. So they readily fell under the sway of his magnetic personality.

Aaron was the trusted helper of Moses, and as long as he was willing to be only a helper he got along all right. It was when he undertook to fill the place of Moses that he failed. Moses went up into the mountain with God and was absent forty days, and Aaron was left in charge. The sublime spectacle of Sinai had just passed. Jehovah had spoken from the mountain, robed in smoke, crowned with fire, and vibrant with thunder. Aaron and all Israel had trembled before it, and entered into a covenant with the God who had spoken from the flame.

However, Moses was gone and Aaron was worried. Somehow, it was not difficult to manage the crowd when Moses was there; now they were restless and discontented. They did not know what was the matter, but they were missing the stalwart personality of Moses and the grip of his strong hand upon the reins. Any people in their situation needed someone to tell them what to do, and Aaron did not know. He was just a bit too proud to follow out the careful directions of Moses, and Moses was not there to tell him.

Aaron had been left to keep things straight, while Moses was getting further instructions from Jehovah; but Aaron was not big enough to meet the occasion, and the people were not able to endure the strain of forty days and nights without a real leader. They had been accustomed all their lives to have their masters tell them what to do, and they soon forgot all their vows before the smoking mount. The greatness and glory of the first two of the Ten Commandments were lost sight of, and they thronged about Aaron, saying, "Up, make us gods, which shall go before us; as for this Moses, the man who brought us out of the land of Egypt, we know not what has become of him" (Exod. 32:1).

Aaron was bewildered. He was not big enough to tell the people to keep faith and wait for Moses; he must do some-

thing and show them that he could lead. It is a mark of
mediocrity for one to be ignorant of his own limitations. We
have reason to think that Aaron wanted to be true to Jehovah
and his great brother, but he was too weak to run the risk of
losing his popularity by going against the multitude. It was
clearly "vox populi," and Aaron was politician enough to pre-
tend that it was "vox dei." Majorities are not always right;
in fact, most of the progress of earth has come through
minorities who suffered and witnessed until the throng came
to appreciate their visions. Moses was most of the time in the
minority, as far as Israel was concerned.

Pleasing People Rather Than God

Aaron was not made of martyr stuff, and he broke under
the strain. Here was his one great chance to play the man,
but although he knew better he most cowardly did the worst.
The golden earrings were gathered and melted into a mass.
Then Aaron with graving tools shaped it into a calf. The
covenant was broken! The second commandment was forgotten! Israel had forsaken Jehovah and turned back to the
bestial idolatry of Egypt. Poor ignorant Israel! Poor weak
Aaron! Less than forty days under Aaron and the people were
spiritually back in the land of bondage. Listen to Aaron,
"Tomorrow is a feast unto Jehovah." What a subterfuge and
tragedy! Abe Lincoln is said to have remarked to a fellow
who was using confusing terms in an argument, "If you call
a calf's tail a leg, how many legs has the calf?"

"Five," answered the opponent.

"You are wrong," said Abe, "calling a tail a leg does not
make it one."

Calling that scene a feast unto Jehovah did not change the
fact that it was a heathen revel. They rose up early in the
morning and made their offerings, and the record says that

they "sat down to eat and drink, and rose up to play." The word translated "play" seems to indicate that their feast was followed by some of the foul orgies which polluted much of the heathen worship of that time. Alas for Aaron, this was no place for mediocrity, no time for a man seeking popularity! Only the strictest loyalty to truth and their covenant with Jehovah could impress those undisciplined hordes—only a few months from brick kilns of Egypt. Aaron could do nothing but hope for Moses, and yet one would hardly think he wanted to see him just then.

The great leader came down from the mount aflame with holy indignation against the sin which not only corrupted the multitude but had basely broken the holy covenant. Moses was almost crushed; he denounced and punished their sin without mercy; yet at the same time he pleaded their case before Jehovah with an earnestness and self-forgetfulness without parallel in history. I rather suspect that you might have heard some simpering Israelite say, "Isn't it a pity that Moses is not a man of broad human sympathy like Aaron?" It is a sad fact that poor, sinful humanity has never been able to know its real friends. Athens gave the hemlock to Socrates and Jerusalem crucified Jesus. It was Aaron who weakly allowed the nation to drift into sin, and it was Moses who punished their sin unsparingly. Yet it was Moses who put himself between them and the wrath of God, crying, "Yet now, if thou wilt forgive their sin—; and if not, blot me, I pray thee, out of thy book which thou hast written" (Exod. 32:32).

Aaron never saw the day that he loved Israel well enough to pray a prayer like that. It took real bigness and measureless love to intercede after that fashion. He was not brave enough to meet the pain and reproach in the face of Moses. Cowardlike, he tried to shield himself by blaming the people.

"Let not the anger of my lord wax hot: thou knowest the people, that they are set on evil. For they said unto me, Make us gods, which shall go before us; for as for this Moses, the man that brought us up out of the land of Egypt, we know not what is become of him. And I said unto them, Whosoever hath any gold, let them break it off: so they gave it to me; and I cast it into the fire, and there came out this calf" (Exod. 32:22–24). Poor lying excuse! It speaks much for the love and forbearance of Moses that he answered with no word of censure. He knew the falsity of Aaron's statement, but possibly he could not trust himself to speak, lest he say too much and make a perpetual breach between them.

It is worthy of note that the only words of the eloquent Aaron which are preserved in the Bible are those of this falsehood about the golden calf. All of his fair words, all of his excellencies of speech availed nothing when strength of character was wanting! Shakespeare says of one of his characters, "Courage mounteth with occasion." Great men meet great problems with courage and strength. Unmoved by triumph or disaster, they "treat those two imposters just the same."

A High Priest; Not a Prophet

And yet, while not one of the royally great, Aaron had many noble qualities. He was just not big enough to rise alone to the heights of the mighty times in which he lived. He would have looked bigger away from Moses and in another day. He was one of the good-meaning men who always need a stronger personality on which to lean. The Aarons are not altogether unworthy; they are just not big enough to be great. They make splendid helpers for bigger men, but are not equal to facing crucial hours alone.

The man whom God chose for the first high priest of Israel must have had many noble traits of head and heart. It does not take as big a man to be a priest as it does to be a prophet. A priest follows rules and rituals; his work is marked out for him. The prophet must see and speak for God ahead of his day, and live above the people about him; and that is manful, testing work. Aaron stayed loyally by Moses, save in the incident of the golden calf and the one brief hour when he and Miriam chafed under the domination of the younger brother, and he followed faithfully and obeyed unquestioningly. Aaron was not big like Moses. Moses was cast in the mold of the Titans. God threw away the patterns when He made Moses and Paul. Our world has too many little men to bear more of them.

Some men are born with a touch of the politician about them; it belongs to the very essence of their nature. It is instinctive with them to seek popularity, and win the favor of the multitude; and yet some of them have rendered wonderful service. Obadiah could live in the house of Ahab, listen to all the mummeries of the priests of Baal, know all the sensuality of their idolatry, and yet not desert Jehovah. He could walk quietly in the midst of this pollution, and at the same time risk his life feeding the persecuted prophets of Jehovah. Elijah could no more have done that than Obadiah could have triumphed on Carmel. All men are not virile like Moses and Elijah, so God uses the weaker men and makes them better as they serve.

Aaron was Israel's first high priest, and right well he filled that holy office. Unflinchingly, he stood by Moses in many a dark hour, sharing his burdens, his praise and his blame. When the murmurers would have killed Moses, they generously included Aaron in the program. Worn-out at last by strenuous toil and the weight of years, the great high priest climbed the majestic heights of Mount Hor and died, with only his brother, his son and his God as pallbearers.

He wore without stain or reproach the robes of a mighty and revered priesthood; and his dust, like that of his greater brother, sleeps in a mountain mausoleum, no man knowing the place, and God alone guarding the secret well.

"In the shroud of the rock they gently wound him,
  'Tis a Bethel pillow that love has given;
I see no gloom of the grave around him,
  The death-bed fetters have all been riven.
'Tis the angel of life not of death that has found him,
  And this is to him the gate of heaven.

"He has seen the tombs of old Mizraim's wonder,
  Where the haughty Pharaohs embalmed recline;
But no pyramid with its costly grandeur,
  Can once be compared with his mountain shrine.
No monarch of Memphis is swathed in splendor,
  High priest of the desert, like this of thine."

References: Exodus, chapters 4 to 8, 16, 28 to 32; Numbers; Acts 7:40; Hebrews 5:4; 7:11.

Balaam

THE MAN OF CONTRADICTIONS

THE Bible is true to human nature. That is one reason why its characters are not consistent. A fully consistent man or woman has never lived. To be consistent, a bad man would have to be bad all the time; and a good man would never be mastered by any evil tendencies. The struggle between the bad within and about us, and the good from without that would lift us out of and above ourselves, makes human nature a bundle of incongruities. God's people will be consistent when they get to heaven, for then nature and environment will fully harmonize.

The final doom of sin is that when fully grown the lost are completely bad and will remain so forever. The contradictions of human nature will end in eternity, when the struggle between good and evil in the souls of men is over forever. If the Bible were to portray perfectly consistent lives, we would need no further evidence of its falsity.

Among all the unusual characters delineated in the Bible, there is none more strikingly contradictory than that of Balaam, the son of Beor. Here we have a man who talked like an angel and plotted like a demon; one who was fully conscious of the power and goodness of Jehovah, and yet loved the "wages of unrighteousness" to his undoing.

Balaam had his high hours when he really wanted to follow Jehovah, of whom he had a conception above many. There were hours when his soul thrilled with the thought of service to an infinite and holy God. It was in such a moment that he said, "If Balak would give me his house full of silver and gold, I cannot go beyond the commandment of the LORD, to do either good or bad of mine own mind; but what the LORD saith, that will I speak" (Num. 24:13). A similar mood must have possessed him when he cried, "Let me die the death of the righteous, and let my last end be like his" (Num. 23:10)! But Balaam had other hours when greed and ambition mastered him.

Robert Louis Stevenson in that wonderful little book, "The Strange Case of Dr. Jekyl and Mr. Hyde," drew that vivid and awful picture of the struggle between the good and the evil in a human soul. In that volume he tells that weird story of a polished and kindly physician who had discovered a drug which enabled him to change both form and character, and become an uncouth and brutal frequenter of dens of vice. As Dr. Jekyl, he was a kindly, useful and altogether admirable member of society; as Mr. Hyde, he was cruel, vicious, low and sensual. This story is only partially true to life. Every man has within him the possibilities of both Dr. Jekyl and Mr. Hyde, and no drug is needed to work the subtle change. The virus of sin in every human heart will transform any man into something like Mr. Hyde, if allowed to work its course unhindered. Also, any human life may be made glorious by the transforming power of the redeeming and renewing gospel of Christ.

This gives us the key to the conduct of Balaam. He knew something of the character and service of Jehovah, and was moved by a desire to follow Him. At the same time, he was influenced by the enchantments and magical rites of the heathen among whom he lived; and at times was completely dominated by his lust for material rewards. His imagination had been caught by the doctrine of the one true God of majesty and holiness, and he was willing to serve Him if the price were not too great. Along with that, however, he had the heathen idea of bribing God to allow him to have his way, and get the gain for which his earthly nature clamored.

Not a True Servant of God

The story of his going with the messengers of Balak is the tale of a man who wanted the favor of the Lord, and at the same time the "wages of unrighteousness." He tried to hold with one hand the good will of the God of Israel and with the other the rewards of Moab. It is the story of a man at war within himself. He is afraid to go against the word of Jehovah, yet all the time he has an eye turned toward the rewards of wickedness. He uttered many noble sentiments and spoke words that were according to the will of God, yet most of them were uttered with a longing in his heart for the fleshpots of earth. He assured Balak that all his wealth would not tempt him to disobey the command of the most High, and at the same time he was trying to persuade God to allow him to accede to the king's request and receive the promised reward. Like Reuben, his was the curse of a double heart. At no time was he fully surrendered to the will of God. He feared Jehovah and the dread of His power made him unwilling to disobey flatly; but all the time he cherished the low concept that by sacrifices and gifts he might bring God to allow that which had been forbidden.

Balaam had some idea of the future life with its sanctions and rewards, else how can we explain his desire to die the death of the righteous. "The death of the righteous," he cried with a longing heart. "The clear conscience, the easy pillow, the untroubled heart of the godly man when the end comes," was his wish. Listening to this, one might count Balaam among the saints, for these words have a heavenly sound. But all of Balaam is not speaking here; there is another window to his soul, and we must peep through it if we would see the whole of the man.

Let us take a good look at this man. He had clearer ideas of God than most men of his day. Sometimes he seems swept into ecstasy, as he muses upon the greatness and glory of the eternal Jehovah; and yet deep in his heart he is planning how he may serve both God and Balak. The man whom Stevenson delineated found that as the days went by it was easier to become Mr. Hyde and more increasingly difficult to return to Dr. Jekyl. Just so, Balaam found that while he said beautiful things about Jehovah, it was becoming harder all the time to relinquish the "wages of unrighteousness."

Things Which Balaam Coveted

What were the things which Balaam coveted? They were the gold of Balak, the life of ease which it would bring, and the promotion and honor which he hoped to have among the princes of Midian. Balaam knew very well that if he went all the way with Jehovah he must bid good-bye to the treasure and preferments of the king. There are plenty of people who would be saints if there was no self-denial in doing right. The Balaams of earth would all be happy if they might have the blessing of God along with the gold of Moab. It would not be hard to be good if the allurements of the world were not so attractive and its gold did not gleam so brightly. They want both; they want to serve God and fool Balak just a little. "Let me die the death of the righteous, but let me also taste the sweets of sin," is their cry.

Poor Balaam! In trying to hold both, he lost both. The devil bought Balaam cheap; he really did not pay anything; he never delivered the promised wages because he could not. Not even the subtlety of Satan can give a man joy with the "wages of unrighteousness." There is no man so foolish as the one who tries to ignore the fact that the laws of the universe are just and holy. One cannot walk with God and the devil at the same time; he cannot load the dice in the game of life.

Balaam tried to serve two masters, and found that one of them could not pay what he promised; and the other would not accept his insincerity. He was not altogether pleased with the service of Jehovah; his nature rebelled against self-denial; the call of the flesh and the world was strong; he felt that he could not afford to miss the favor of Balak, but he was afraid of Jehovah. He thought that if he would offer many sacrifices maybe God would allow him the treasure which his heart coveted. In his cupidity, he fondly imagined God to be like unto himself, and felt that possibly he might purchase his indulgence. When a man thinks like that, he may look with longing eyes toward the death of the righteous, but the dangling, glittering baits of the devil will lure him into devious and crooked paths. Such a man is much more likely to die alongside Evi, Rekem, Zur and Hur, the princes of Midian than to ride in Elijah's chariot.

No man in English history wrote more charmingly of the beauty of virtue and the value of integrity than Francis Bacon; yet he, too, loved the "wages of unrighteousness," and flirted with temptation until his light flickered out in the darkness. The son of Beor was by no means the last man to talk like an angel and sin like a fiend of the pit. Not all of his class are hypocrites; they are not consciously playing a part. They have hours when they appreciate the better things, and make themselves believe they are serving God; and then there are days when the Mr. Hyde of their nature asserts himself and they revel in the "wages of unrighteousness." Such men deceive themselves into thinking they can have both the favor of God and the delights of sinful pleasure. They tell the

tempter that a house filled with his treasures would not lead
them astray, and at the same time they build their seven
altars, hoping that God will allow them the treasures of
Midian. Jehovah cannot be bought, and gold is a mighty de-
ceptive thing; and the man who continues to look upon it
with greedy eyes will find himself plotting the vileness of
Shittim while reaching for the forbidden fruit.

Some Important Lessons to Learn

There are some plain and simple lessons to be learned from
the story of Balaam.

One of them is that the garb and name of a prophet is no
guarantee of the real life of the man. Some of the worst men
of history have worn priestly robes, but have hidden under
pious platitudes ways that are dark and tricks worthy of the
prince of rascals. No one complained that Judas was not a
good preacher. For ought we know he was more popular
with the crowd than Peter or John. There are some puzzling
things about Balaam. It is hard to tell just how he stood
before God. Some men have gone to heaven who have done
very wicked and foolish things. If Balaam was saved, it was
a miracle of divine grace; and when we think about it rightly,
it is so with all of us. But whatever we may say, his reputa-
tion for religion did not save him from divine displeasure
when he went wrong. There is no exemption clause in the
moral laws for preachers or religious leaders; they cannot
hanker after the forbidden things without moral deteriora-
tion.

Another thing we learn is that there must be no double mind
in the service of God. We cannot have both the favor of the
Lord and the gain of sin; we can choose which we will have,
but most certainly we cannot have both. Balaam seemed to
think that his worship of God and his daily life lay in different

fields, and that by sacrifices and gifts God might be brought to allow him to do as he wished. He was not the first man, nor by any means the last man who has endeavored to make his daily life and his Christian service things apart. God and mammon can no more dwell in the same heart now than in the days of Jesus. Church membership and the observance of ordinances will never sweeten a life that seeks to garner the "wages of unrighteousness" from the oppression of the poor, or from crooked business or machine politics.

Men cannot rob dishonest gain of its ugliness in the sight of God by dropping something in a collection plate or giving to some popular charity. Christ must have all of a man's life or He will have none of it. There is no twilight zone where one may reap the fruits of sin, while he appeases God by gifts or formal worship in His house. Cardinal Wolsey, no doubt, meant to be a good man, but he could not be true to God and serve the sensual schemes and unholy ambitions of Henry the VIII. He could see the rewards of Henry and was not strong enough to resist, so he tried to fool God and failed.

Our Bible is a book of inflexible honesty; to follow it one must be honest with God, with his fellows and with himself. It insists that the new life in Christ shall go down to the very roots of our being; and if there is anything hidden or that is not straight, it is displeasing to God. The Balaams, who have corners in their souls where they feast upon the "wages of unrighteousness" while they shut God out, are going to be terribly shocked when they meet His inexorable judgments.

Again, the great fact is that the best things of life are not won by simply wishing for them. Balaam was sincere in his wish to die the death of the righteous, but one must have more than a wishbone to attain those things. The world has many people who want the cloudless sky and the light that beckons the good man when the long shadows of life are cast eastward;

yet at the same time they are bidding for the favor of Balak
and the gold of Moab while this life lasts. All such will fail
where Balaam failed and have an end like his.

When Israel came to number the slain on that fateful day,
when they avenged the foul seductions of Midian, they found
among the bodies of the foes of God the cold form of the
desert prophet. He doubtless garnered the gold of Balak, but
failed to die the death of which he sang so sweetly. Poor
man! He wore a prophet's robe, yet was so greedy of gold
that he was more stupid than the beast on which he rode;
and he learned that the "wages of unrighteousness" will not
mingle with divine benedictions. Seeking the reward of both
God and Balak, he won neither. Dreaming of the triumphant
death of a good man, while clinging to the rewards of sin,
he lost all. His death was violent and shameful, and the wages
for which he longed were such as he could not carry on his
long and hurried journey.

References: Numbers, chapters 22–24; 31:8, 16; II Peter 2:15; Jude 11;
Revelation 2:14.

Shamgar

THE HERO OF THE OX GOAD

SHAMGAR does not have much space in the Bible. However, that wonderful Book can say so much in a few words, that simply to be named there is to be on time's honor roll. The Spartans, we are told, delighted in those terse, pithy sentences which came to be known as "laconic." The Bible is a laconic book; it can sum up the history of a mighty life in one brief sentence. A whole cyclopedia could tell no more than it does about Enoch, and it uses only four short verses. There is only one verse about Shamgar; just a few words tell all we need to know. The name of Shamgar is among the great men of sacred story, yet we do not know where he lived, or how long he lived; not even the name of the tribe to which he belonged is given.

Still, we know a lot about Shamgar. We know that he lived in troublous times, in a day when Israel was unfortunate. It was the period just after the greatness of Moses. Joshua and his immediate successors had passed. The mountains had shrunk into foothills, and the foothills had flattened out into a barren plain, with here and there a little hillock. Ehud and Othniel had gone, and Deborah and Gideon had not yet come. Israel had forgotten her troubles and her need of Jehovah at the same time. The Philistines, those ugly neighbors of Israel, had just appeared on the scene. The forms of heathen worship about them looked mighty attractive, and they had grown tired of the strictness of the law of Moses.

At this time, the Philistines came along. There is always

a Philistine of some sort to worry the backslidden children of God. These Philistines were a fighting crowd. Israel at her best always had her hands full when dealing with these warriors from the coast country. Only little bands of them invaded the land at first; but when they found no organized opposition they came in greater numbers. They plundered the people, burned their homes, and wrought general havoc. The conditions were horrible. The Israelites were completely cowed and were at the mercy of their cruel foes. The villages were sacked, the property that could be carried away was taken, the children carried into slavery, and the fairest girls taken to the harems of their masters. Weeds, bushes and briars covered the fields, and a somber cloud of ruin hung over the land. The burly Philistine strutted down the highway, and the Israelite hid when he saw him coming.

Here and there was an Israelite who tried to keep on working. No doubt Shamgar belonged to this class. All he wanted was to keep his home and avoid trouble. Shamgar was not a professional fighter; he was a worker, and fighting was not his business. If you had been looking for someone to lead the fight against the invader, you would not have picked Shamgar. He was not prepared to fight; he had no armour, no sword, no spear; in fact, he had none of the equipment which a fighter thinks he needs. You could hardly imagine a man more poorly fitted to deal with those warlike invaders. Then, Shamgar was busy; he was out in the fields trying to make a living. His hands knew the feel of the plow and the pruning hook, and were rough and horny from honest toil.

When the Saint Should Fight

We do not know what brought Shamgar into the fight—the record does not say. We are sure that he did not want to fight; he would have been a splendid pacifist if the Philistines had just stayed at home where they belonged. He was of the same school as Sergeant York of World War fame; he did not want to fight and did not believe in fighting. However, fellows of that class make wonderful soldiers when the provocation becomes sufficient.

Every day, when Shamgar went out to his work, he saw some new outrage which had been perpetrated; some home had been burned, or some poor woman came to him with the story of her children who had been carried away into something worse than death. He saw the sons of the giants stalking through the land, and his own people skulking behind hedgerows and in the out-of-the-way places. No doubt, Shamgar thought much about such conditions, and brooded deeply over the way things were going. We may believe, though the Bible does not say, that Shamgar kept up the worship of Jehovah. Somewhere, there was a lonely altar where he worshiped the God of Abraham and Isaac and Jacob. God finds His Shamgars among the praying men of the world; in fact, he can find them nowhere else.

One morning Shamgar went out to his work as usual, driving his oxen yoked to a rude plow, and carrying his old goad in his hand. The Philistines did something worse than usual that morning. Maybe they invaded his home and tried to abuse his family. Possibly they tried to seize his oxen. It might have been the sight of some deed of unusual cruelty upon some of his neighbors. At least, it was more than Shamgar could bear, and he swung that ox goad against a very hateful Philistine. Almost to the surprise of the old plowman, the invader went down to stay and Shamgar was an outlaw.

There are worse things than being an outlaw; it all depends upon the conditions. David was an outlaw under Saul. All that kept Washington, John Adams and Patrick Henry from being outlaws was the fact that they succeeded. Likely there were other Philistines in that gang, and the comrades of the dead man went after the Hebrew who had slain their fellow. Now an ox goad is not mentioned among the approved weapons of war, but it did splendid execution that day, and there were more dead Philistines. Just a brawl, one might say, but things like that have started movements that changed the map of the world. It was some peasants defending their homes that set in motion the struggle for the freedom of Switzerland; and the Boston massacre and the defense of the Alamo would have been no more than brawls, if they had not started wars that made history.

It had been a long time since the people of Israel had seen a dead Philistine, and they suddenly realized that their tyrants were mortal. The Philistines soon came back with a bigger body of soldiers; they wanted the head of that obstreperous Hebrew. By this time a little company of Hebrews had gathered behind the shaggy Shamgar and his goad. It is wonderful how even the most ordinary folk will pluck up courage when a real leader comes on the scene. The die was cast and Shamgar must win or die, and he did not want to die—just then. The blood of the plowman was up, and the wrongs of all the years were throbbing in his brain and burning in his veins. The neighbors were seeing a new Shamgar. None of them would have thought this plain farmer was such a fighter. He had no sword, no shield, not a shred of armour, just his rude goad, its point now reddened with the blood of the oppressor.

The Philistines came merrily up the highway; they would make short work of this presumptuous upstart. They had been accustomed to having their way in the land of Israel; but somehow the ox goad in the hands of this aroused stalwart was a more deadly weapon than the best of their swords and spears. Before they hardly knew what had happened, they were racing for the border, leaving more of their number on the ground.

The Weak Are Made Strong

How the news spread over the land! The Philistines had been routed! A new leader had arisen in the tribes of Israel! The old battle cry of the nation, "To your tents, O Israel," was heard again; and seizing such crude weapons as they could find, the sons of Jacob charged home upon the foe. All the while, just in front of the foremost was the husky form of Shamgar. The first weapon to taste blood was the same old goad which had prodded the sluggish oxen along many a weary mile. Just an ox goad—but ox goads, plus Shamgars, are dangerous weapons of war! Give us a Shamgar and we will find you a victory—no matter whether he be clad in armour or must snatch his weapons from the rude implements of toil! You must not think of the ox goad alone but of Shamgar and his God, for he who wields an ox goad on God's side will find God by his side.

"What is in thine hand, Moses?"

"Just a rod, the plain old staff which I have carried for twenty years to divide the sheep from the goats."

"God wants you, Moses; wants you just as you are. You must tackle Pharaoh barehanded; bring your rod and come along."

With nothing but a rod in his hand, Moses was bigger than any Egyptian monarch that ever lived, backed by all the hosts of the valley of the Nile.

"What is in thine hand, Abraham Lincoln?"

"Just the training of a rail splitter, a handful of books, a few law books, a copy of Shakespeare, Pilgrim's Progress, and a Bible."

"Bring the ox goad and come along; things are going to happen. Millions of slaves must be freed, and a mighty nation must pass through the fires."

Just another ox goad, but Lincoln with his shaggy hair, his uncouth form and his simple speech proved to be the man for the darkest hour that America had known.

"What have you in your hand, D. L. Moody? How much training have you had?"

"Just enough to read and write, but my heart yearns over the millions who are lost; I think of them day and night."

"Come along! God wants another Shamgar. Will you come?"

"Yes, Lord, I will give you all that I have. The sword is mighty dull and the scabbard is old-fashioned, but you may have all of it from hilt to point."

The modern Shamgar came, and the shouts of the saints and the songs of the newly-born were heard on two continents, as a mighty revival was felt in the English-speaking world.

Use the Talents You Possess

Shamgar, the hero of the ox goad, wrote his name in the annals of the chosen people. History would read differently without the Shamgars. Suppose the ox-driver had said, "If I just had a new sword and a good suit of armour, I would start something." There would have been no deliverance, and sorrow would have mantled Israel until God could find another man. There are times when to be unprepared is a crime. We ought always to use the very best that God allows us to have. But when the foe is mighty and the invaders from the five cities trample upon the Canaan of God, there may be no time to wait for sword or spear. Then come, Shamgar! We will follow you! We will follow you despite your uncut hair, your plow shoes and your awkward stride. You are God's man! Any fellow who will face the mail-clad Philistines with only an ox goad is worthy to be followed.

Some of us who have all that the schools can give have never seen the backs of our foes. We have been dalliers and cowards, while the Shamgars with their rough hands and shabby clothes have written their names among those who "have delivered Israel." God had a place for Saul of Tarsus, polished like a Damascus blade, and a mighty big place it was. He also has a place for the man with nothing but an ox goad, and such have wrought mightily in His kingdom.

Let every man use the best that God has given him or will enable him to get, but the workman must be bigger than his tools and the soldier must be keener than his blade. The soul must glow more brightly than the polished blade, and a real man must fill the burnished armour. A throbbing heart must make the words burn, if men are to be moved to action and the Philistines are to be conquered. Better one Shamgar than a thousand whining cowards, waiting for something to turn up. God and Shamgar will win over any odds. The Philistines dread the Shamgars; they know that such men are invincible. Just an ox-driver who heard the voice of God! May his tribe increase, for he "also delivered Israel."

> Come, Shamgar, with your shaggy hair,
>   Your heavy, awkward stride;
> A man the warriors down in Gath
>   Will mimic and deride.
> Come, Shamgar, with your rustic form,

Come leave the axe and plow;
The sons of Anak walk the land,
    And Israel needs you now.

"I have no sword or armour bright,
    No mace nor pointed spear;
The only weapon to my hand,
    This rusty ox goad here."
Philistines trample through the land
    To rob and burn and slay,
No time to wait for sword and shield,
    Come quickly, Shamgar, pray!

The plowman came with goad in hand,
    A rude, heroic soul,
And they have writ old Shamgar's name
    On Israel's honor roll.
Such as he had, he freely gave,
    His strength and weapons rude;
Where soldiers failed he held the field,
    And won a nation's gratitude.

When leaders blench and armies fail,
    And martial gear is not,
Do not despair for God may send
    Some Shamgar to the spot.
For willing hands and flaming hearts
    Are more than armour bright,
And goads in Shamgars' stalwart hands
    Will turn to day the night.

References: Judges 3:31; 5:6.

Deborah

A NEW WOMAN OF YE OLDEN TIME

Sometimes the best man in a country is a woman and, when that happens, all the laws and regulations which men have made will not keep her from running things. This has been true in all history. Maria Theresa was queen and wore the purple right royally. There were many men in Merry England in the days of good Queen Bess, and they all took orders from her. It was even so in Palestine in the days of the judges.

Things were in a bad way when Deborah came upon the scene. Israel did not have a man who was equal to the emergency in the life of the nation. Jabin and Sisera were masters of the land, and they ruled it to the serfdom of Israel. The governors lived in Machur, and there were literary men in Zebulun, but they were worthless when it came to freeing their land from its oppressors. Reuben did a lot of thinking but stayed with the bleating of the sheep. Gilead remained in the eastern hills beyond Jordan, while Dan took to the ships along the coast, and Asher hid in the narrow valleys where the mountains met the sea.

The cry went up for a man, a real, sure-enough man. The Ehuds with daggers in their left hands were gone, and there were no more rugged Shamgars with their deadly ox goads. This was a time when they believed that a woman was very much the inferior of man; and it is proof of the low estate into which the country had fallen that they were willing to listen to a woman.

We know very little about brother Lapidoth, the husband of our heroine; he was doubtless a pretty good sort of man, and the best thing we know about him is that he did not try to manage Deborah. When a man is weak and negative, and a woman is strong and positive, she will be the real head of the house. He may seem to be filling the position, but the woman knows that he is not, and the public usually finds it out. Many a wife pulls the strings which make her husband seem to be a big man, but it is most generally known who is the power behind the throne. Thank God for such a woman when the men fail. God will put a man in the lead if He can find one who is strong in faith and humble in spirit, but if not there is room for a Deborah.

The little villages in Israel were empty; the people of the land had fled from the robbers and brigands, who called themselves the soldiers of Jabin, and dwelt in the woods and caves. It was a desolate land whose people were completely subdued, a people without weapons and without courage. It looked like a hopeless task for the strongest man, let alone a woman. Ehud and Shamgar had gained victories, but they were big, burly men with strong bodies and brawny arms. Yet something had to be done, and the woman under the palm tree heard the call, "Awake, Deborah, awake!" When Deborah answered, things began to happen.

Barak meant "lightning," but he did not flash very much nor strike very hard unless Deborah was by his side. Some modern women think they have to crowd men out to show what they can do, but this ancient heroine was perfectly willing that Barak should have the glory of the campaign; but when he was not big enough to go alone, she went along and the Lord gave her the credit to which she was entitled. Deborah was one of those who had greatness thrust upon her; circumstances made her a leader in a crucial hour.

God Looks for a Man and Finds a Woman

Israel was in the midst of one of their periodic backslidings. For twenty years the iron chariots of Jabin had rumbled through a subject land. Those Hebrews just would tamper with forbidden fruit and go after false gods. God had been raising up champions for them, but this time no deliverer came. God could find no man in all Israel, so He called a woman. Deborah was married, but Lapidoth seems to have had the good sense to stay in the background and let Deborah work out her own problems.

Deborah was already a judge in Israel,—"And she dwelt under the palm tree of Deborah between Ramah and Bethel in mount Ephraim: and the children of Israel came up to her for judgment" (Judges 4:5).

Now this tells more than appears at first sight. It was no common woman to whom a nation brought their disputes for settlement, in a time when mere masculinity was a badge of superiority. No weakling could have so commanded the respect and confidence of a disorderly and unorganized people. They not only respected her judgment, but they trusted her integrity. People do not voluntarily submit to an arbiter in whom they have no confidence.

It is something of an innovation at the present time when a woman dons the ermine and deals out even-handed justice in the courts of the land; yet more than three thousand years ago this capable woman was the highest court of appeal in the Hebrew nation. There was no law compelling them to submit their disputes to her for settlement; they came of their own free will to lay their legal problems at the feet of this remarkable woman. It must have been a busy place under the old palm tree, as the quarrels and differences of the whole people were settled according to the words of Deborah. There is no record of complaint, and we may believe that she made things so clear and plain that the litigants went away content. While some were ignorant through sloth and some by necessity, Deborah was an authority upon the laws of Israel. The last word of justice in the land was given by this clear-eyed woman, holding court under the old palm tree.

There was a total absence of legal pomp and dignity; there were no arched chambers and long halls with dim windows; everything was in the open. Deborah was just a motherly woman sitting under a palm tree; her whole equipment was a copy of the law of Jehovah and judgment was rendered according to its precepts. An entire nation sat at the feet of this unusual woman. Deborah and her palm tree have their place in the history of jurisprudence, and we must recognize her powers of mind and heart.

Deborah was more than a judge; she was a prophet of Jehovah. She was one who waited upon Him and through whom the Spirit spoke. It took real stuff to remain true to Israel's God and speak for Him, while the nation was walking in strange paths and worshiping other deities. Say what we please about the place of woman, the fact remains that God has spoken through them, and when men have failed He has used them to carry out His plans. It was a woman who kept the Word of Jehovah in the land during that dark day of wicked backsliding. Maybe God intended that women should always be in the background, but here is Deborah and she will require a lot of explaining. She was not in the rear ranks, and she was by no means silent; she was the most potent force in Israel for fifty years.

It was no accident that the movement for the restoration of Hebrew independence began under that palm tree. There was no other place in Israel with enough vision and courage for such work to begin. Those who believe in God and stand for His law have always been the champions of freedom.

When Jesus said, "One is your Master, even Christ; and all ye are brethren," He sounded the death knell of every unjust autocracy upon earth. It was Deborah, prophetess and judge, who raised the cry of defiance against the oppressor and brought a revival of hope to the nation. She sent for Barak, evidently a man of note, whom she felt the people would follow. She promised him victory, if he would gather an army and lead them out by Mount Tabor, but Barak was not big enough and brave enough to be the champion of Israel. Deborah tried mighty hard to make a national hero of the man from Kedesh-naphthali, but he was not made of hero stuff and will have to go down in history as one of the near paladins.

Accordingly, Deborah had to enter new fields and add the martial skill of the warrior to the piety of the prophet and the dignity of a judge. This most extraordinary woman combined in herself many of the qualities of greatness. She had the moral grandeur of a Samuel, the legal lore of an Ezra, and the courage of Joan of Arc. Let the next man to speak lightly of the ability of women to lead and rule take time to consider Deborah.

Laborers Together With God

Barak rode at the head of the army, but Deborah was the real leader; she told him just what to do and how to do it. The plain people of Israel were not fooled; they knew who was the deliverer of the nation, and they honored Deborah as their emancipator. Poor Barak lost the name that might have been his, and the name of another woman, Jael the wife of Heber, the slayer of Sisera, was renowned in song and story. Great victory came through the planning of Deborah; the stars in their courses fought with the children of Israel. The victory was complete, the oppressors were routed, the

land was free, and the hearts of the people turned back to
Jehovah. There was more involved than just their deliverance
from subjugation; there was a moral renovation of the
people. Deborah had been used by Jehovah, not only to free
them from cruel tyranny but also to lead them back to the
God of their fathers.

When this was done, Deborah revealed another element of
greatness and added the bay wreath of the poet to the renown
of the warrior and rectitude of the judge. The record says
that Deborah and Barak sang the song recorded in the fifth
chapter of Judges. The poem reveals, however, that while
Barak may have added his bass to the singing, that the words
are those of Deborah. It is a remarkable psalm of rejoicing
over a wonderful deliverance and a worthy tribute of praise
to Jehovah for His avenging of Israel. It is filled with beautiful commendations and deft rebuke.

How cogently stated are the words of praise for the governors of Israel who offered themselves willingly, and how
keen the irony of reproof for the Danites sheltered from the
battle in their ships, and Gilead hiding in the mountains.
There is unusual beauty in the glowing lines about the heroism
of Zebulun and Naphtali, and the scathing denunciation of
Meroz has become a classic wherever the Bible is read. There
was iron at white heat in the soul of the singer, as she looked
upon the smug complacency of that sheltered hamlet which
was coolly unconcerned while others fought and bled for
freedom. The lightning flashed and the deep roll of thunder
echoed as she poured forth that withering curse upon the
people who failed in that crucial hour.

In the anthology of verse for all time there must be a niche
for Deborah, who sang the praise of Jehovah and poured the
tide of approval upon the heroes of that day, while she

stamped the names of the lovers of ease with everlasting ignominy.

Those who think that women have only of late come into their own can learn something under the old palm tree between Ramah and Bethel. They might well ponder this woman who led Israel to battle and under whose direction the very stars and rivers played their part. It is nothing new for women to have their place in the affairs of nations. Herodotus tells us of Semiramis and Nitocris, two women who ruled among the Chaldeans while Babylon was in the making. Every student of modern history knows the story of the Catherines of Russia, Margaret of Sweden, and Victoria of England.

When we get uneasy lest women should run away with things and the order of nature be reversed, let us remember that in all history, sacred and profane, they have exerted mighty leadership. In no case where women figured greatly have real men been driven out. After Deborah came Gideon, Jepthah, Samson, and the glory of David and Solomon. Great Britain did not suffer in prestige for the fifty years of Queen Victoria, and her sons and grandsons have not lessened the dignity of their manhood by occupying the same throne.

Deborah, the woman, the wife, the mother in Israel! Deborah, the judge! Deborah, the prophet of God! Deborah, the marshal of the stricken field! Deborah, the poetess! She ranks among the queenly women of all time. Greatness is not a matter of sex. It is all right, at a time when God and His cause need a leader, and no man meets the challenge of the hour, for some Deborah to mount the bench and see that justice does not perish in the land, to seize the sword and when victory is won to write the story in vibrant song.

It will help us to get some things straight about woman's

work, if we will study carefully the career of Deborah. God uses men when they can be found, but He will not let His cause perish because men are cowardly and impotent. He will honor His Deborahs and give them their place among the great of the earth. God never intended that one-half the human race should have no part in the on-going of His kingdom.

> "They talk about a woman's sphere
>   As though it had a limit;
>   There's not a place in earth or heaven,
>   There's not a task to mortals given;
>   There's not a blessing or a woe,
>   There's not a whisper, yes or no,
>   That has a feather's weight of worth
>   Without a woman in it."

References: Judges 4:4–14; 5:1–15.

Eli

A FATHER WHO FAILED

Eli was not a bad man. He was one of the easy-going, good-natured, spineless sort of men. He was one of those about whom the people say, "He hasn't an enemy in the world." This, however, is a mighty sorry endorsement of goodness in a world where the devil has so many disciples, and so many evils are entrenched. No real man wants that epitaph on his tombstone.

> "He has no enemies, you say!
>   My friend the boast is poor.
> He who has mingled in the fray
>   Of duty that the strong endure,
> Must have made foes! If he has none
> Small is the work that he has done:
> He has bit no traitor on the hip,
> He has cast no cup from tempted lip;
> He has never turned the wrong to right,
> He has been a coward in the fight."

Eli was a pretty fair judge. We have no record that he was other than honest and fair in dealing with matters between man and man. He was a good priest, as far as the ordinary duties of his office were concerned. He was doubtless careful and punctilious about the details of his position. The folk who came to Shiloh to worship all liked Eli. He never wounded anybody's conscience, and no one ever had his sins very forcibly brought to mind by Eli. He was worried about wrong, but he would not have made any one uncomfortable about it for the world. In the great things of life he was a failure. I think he was saved; a lot of people are saved "as by fire." Yet as a teacher of righteousness, he allowed the moral sense of the nation to decay under his leadership, and, worst of all, he failed as a father.

There is no greater catastrophe upon earth than that which comes to the father or mother who loses the children whom God has given them. The Christian parents of this world must fight the world, the flesh, and the devil for their children. Satan watches every cradle and lays snares for the feet of every baby that ever was born. About the threshold of every home wages the battle between life and death, and the father and mother who would win the fight must be in grim, dead earnest.

Eli believed in letting things alone. He was one of those who said, "Oh, everything will come out all right." Things have never come out all right of themselves in this world; men have had to "resist unto blood" striving against sin. No field of corn or cotton ever won against briers and weeds when left alone. To neglect things that need attention is the world's way, the easy way, the way of failure. Eli let things alone; he fondly hoped that his boys would get through sowing wild oats and settle down, but he made no effort to discourage their manner of life. The world usually speaks well of the Elis; they are smooth, even folks; they never stir up any trouble. Poor Jeremiah stirred up things and got in jail. They said, "Poor fellow, he was a good man, but you know he was always causing trouble." The fact is that most of the men who have done much for God have stirred up trouble.

"Art thou he that troubleth Israel?" queried the weak and sinful Ahab of the intrepid Elijah.

"Yes, we want a man like Eli; everything goes so smoothly when we have a man like him in the pulpit."

It looked as if things were going well with Eli and his house. He was the high priest, his sons were coming along, and one of them would come into that position when he was gone. Things looked bright for the Eli family.

However, God did not agree with the estimate of the crowd, and He sent a message to Eli about the way things were going. Eli's sons were bad and Eli knew it; he had known it all the while. Eli was one of the "broad-minded" sort of folks—the devil has been an artist in the use of that word "broad-minded." Just let a church member begin to dance, tipple, play cards and play the devil generally, and you will hear him say, "Well, now you know that I am broad-minded." Poor simpleton! He may never in his life have thought any question straight through; he may be thinking all the time of his selfish gratification—but he is "broad-minded." The fact is that such folk are the shallowest, narrowest crowd upon the face of the earth.

Beware of "Broad-minded" Preachers

The most awful, most short-sighted, most foolish thing in all the world is sin, which when reduced to its least common denominator is pure selfishness. The man or woman who lives only to pamper his or her carnal appetite is narrow enough to look through the needle's eye with both eyes without squinting. He is a broad-minded preacher who never rebukes sin. The dancers, the covetous, the dram-drinkers, the crowd who strip themselves as nearly nude as the law will allow in public, all praise the Elis.

It is a poor commendation for a preacher to be popular with

some folks. We read of those in the long ago of whom it was said, "They loved the praise of men more than the praise of God," and that sin was not a monopoly of the ancient Pharisees. Eli was popular with the crowd, but God brought a severe indictment against him. It was a fearful message which He sent by the young Samuel to the old priest. It was a word of rebuke, a verdict of failure, and a warning of coming judgment. "Behold, I will do a thing in Israel, at which both the ears of every one that heareth it shall tingle. In that day I will perform against Eli all things which I have spoken concerning his house: when I begin, I will also make an end. For I have told him that I will judge his house for ever for the iniquity which he knoweth; because his sons made themselves vile, and he restrained them not" (I Sam. 3:11-13). There comes an hour when we cannot dodge, when we must face the judgment of things, and that hour had struck with Eli. He had failed as a moral leader, failed as the head of his nation, and failed in the greatest of human tasks—that of a father.

A man may amass millions; he may hold the most honored positions in the gift of his fellows; but if he has failed in his home, his life is a colossal tragedy. You will notice that God laid the blame upon Eli. Eli was not ignorant of what was going on—"the iniquity which he knoweth." The matter was not hidden from the father, and he knew that it was iniquity. Eli had not been deceived; the true situation was open to him. He knew and yet he either winked at the sin, or was too cowardly and weak to make an effective protest. Possibly he felt that it would hardly be popular to deal with their sins according to law, or he may have said, "I love my sons too well to correct them for their sins as they deserve."

We have all heard of the father and mother who loved their children too well to correct their wrong doing. Such people are sadly mistaken; it is themselves they love. They suffer when their children are disciplined, and they are not willing to be uncomfortable for the sake of the child. This is weakness—sinful and puerile weakness.

Things went from bad to worse with the family of Eli. He remonstrated quietly after a fashion, but that was all. There was no holy purpose in his words, no zeal for right or the honor of Jehovah in what he did. He was a priest in Israel and also a judge. The welfare of the nation and the sanctity of the laws were in his charge. He failed both as a judge and a priest, but greatest of all was his failure as a father. God intends every man to have influence enough and be big enough to hold his home for righteousness. The father who does not have character enough to keep his home from becoming a sink of iniquity has fallen short of being the man God intended him to be.

"He Restrained Them Not"

Restraint is exercised in a thousand ways, but Eli used none of them. We control by what we are, rather than by what we say or do, and what we say and do has weight in proportion to what we are. We must be in dead earnest to make our faith effective, for our children are wonderfully keen to sense the reality of things. If we make our devotion to Christ the big thing of our lives, they will know it, and our influence will be in proportion.

Mere harmlessness is not all there is to being good. A fence post is harmless, but one would hardly call it good. When a man is watching our sheep, and the wolves are threatening, we want him to think enough of sheep to kill the wolves in their defense. We want a man who can shoot and shoot straight. A man who builds a home must be willing to defend that home, or he has no business building one.

The man who wants vice kept out of his home, as badly as the owners of live stock want the wild beasts kept away from their farms, will find some way of doing it.

God expects more of His people than a quiet ignoring of evil. He wants every power of our nature rallied to a stern resistance of sin in every form. Evils are not conquered, devils are not cast out, mighty iniquities are not defeated by letting things alone. All that sin asks is to be let alone. "Let us alone," was the cry of the demons who trembled before our Lord, and it has been the cry of every organized form of evil since. Luther did not let the sale of indulgences alone; he grasped the sword of truth and smote with both hands.

Eli let things alone; he did not want trouble, but letting evil things alone always brings trouble. The liquor traffic, that lusty offspring of the nether regions, has always cried, "Let us alone; you are stirring up trouble," whenever its right to ruin and damn the souls and bodies of men has been questioned. The gambling hell and the house of shame echo the same cry. The forces which oppress the poor and wring wealth from sweat shops have the same pitiful wail. All the false teachers in church and state raise the same old slogan of selfish hypocrisy.

Eli tried that policy out thoroughly, and things went from bad to worse. "He restrained them not." There is something vigorous in that word "restrain"; it has the ring of authority in it. There is some kinship between it and the "Thou shalt nots" of the law of Sinai. God expects restraint. He looked for Eli to set his house in order in the fear of God. The father who evades this God-given task is a coward and a shirker to the nth degree. It is hardly fashionable in these piping times to talk about the control of children and family discipline. We have listened to the silly chatter of that school which teaches that a child must not be restrained, but must be allowed to develop its own personality in its own way. The best answer to this philosophy of ease which ignores evil is found in reformatories and penitentiaries filled with juvenile criminals.

This is the philosophy of ease, the psychology that ignores evil, and would throw off all moral restraints. However, the Bible is an old Book and has been here a long time, and with some of us it is not out of date.

> "A lie whatever the guise it wears,
>   Is a lie as in days of yore;
> But the truth that has stood for a million years,
>   Is good for a million more."

Where Did Eli Fail?

Not in the duties of the priesthood, not in living a clean life, not in kindly remonstrance, but in *discipline*. Now no man has a right to be a tyrant in his home. If he does not have character to control it without a club, he will not do it with one. Not that the right sort of discipline, even chastisement, should be ignored; a good hickory stick rightly applied has been a means of grace to many a youngster at certain periods of his career. It is not a question of how, but of the will to do. Eli was not in blood earnest about things; he did not say they must stop; he just hoped that they might stop. He temporized and shirked, and then looked for the best. He hoped that his sons would leave off some of the things they were doing, but he did not lay himself out to that end.

"Tingling ears," a story of ruin; the enemies of Israel were victorious and the glory of the nation was beaten into the dust; Hophni and Phinehas lay dead upon the trampled field of blood; and Eli was a sprawled and lifeless corpse at Shiloh's gate. The message shattered the hopes of Israel; surely the ears of all who heard it tingled. What lay back of it all? A father had failed; he did not fight sin; he failed to restrain his sons in their wild rush into evil.

This age needs the lesson of Eli. We are impatient of authority. We clamor for the throwing off of restraints, and many of us are ethical anarchists. Reverence for God and holy things is a lost art in all too many of our homes. It is no accident that the leaders of communism and anarchy are atheists. God stands for law and they are lawless. The idea of the Bible means authority, but they want none to interfere with their own desires.

Back of all responsible government lies the real home, and back of the home is God. Folk like Eli are playing with fire, the children are caught in the burning house, and there is no fire department big enough to quench the flames. The poor mother who called her baby "Ichabod" sensed the real truth of things. The glory of the nation had departed; Eli was dead, his sons lay unburied on the field where the soldiers of Israel had fallen, and the ark of God was in the hands of the exultant Philistines. Yes, the good-natured, smooth-spoken and kindly Eli had failed! Failed as the moral leader, failed as God's chosen man, and above all failed as a father. It is failure when one's children forget God, even if there are no stricken fields of death.

Eli was a judge in Israel, but he failed. He wore the pontifical robes of a mighty priesthood, yet he failed. God blamed Eli. Eli had said, "Why do ye such things?" but there was no vigor in his remonstrance. He was a sort of moral pacifist; he kept the peace, but he did not keep much else. Failing in his fatherhood, he failed in everything else. It takes manhood, spirituality and common sense to be a good father. It is a job which calls for all the wisdom, godliness and strength which one can muster.

It was a fearful accounting that came to the house of Eli. The father and sons were bound in one bundle of judgment before God: the sons for their ugly and sacreligious sins, and Eli because he had failed in his authority as the head of his house. He was a judge, but sin went unwhipped and unabashed. He was a father, but allowed his sons who held holy places to lead corrupt lives which he and all Israel knew.

The case of Eli refutes the idea that to be a sort of negative, harmless man, whom all the people like, is enough. Eli was devoted to the tabernacle, and it was when the captivity of the ark was mentioned that the old priest fell from his seat by the gate to his death. To love good things is not enough. Real goodness has red blood and tough muscles; it belongs to the same clan as Bunyan's "Valiant for Truth." God wanted Eli to be a bulwark against the evils that ruined his home and desolated the land, but Eli lacked the fortitude which the hour demanded. One might have written on his tombstone, "A good, harmless man whom everyone liked, but a father who failed."

References: I Samuel, chapters 1 to 4; 14:3; I Kings 2:27.

Hannah

A MOTHER WHO SUCCEEDED

History is made by big men and big men are the sons of great mothers. This has been true all down the ages. There are times in the life of nations when someone has to intervene to start again on the upward path those things which have gone wrong. When the schools have failed, when statesmen have gotten lost in the fog, when preachers can do naught but pray, God starts things in the right direction with a mother. He uses men, but the mother must come along before He can find His man.

The time of Hannah was one of those periods in the career of Israel. The nation was bogged down in the mud and muck of idolatry and sensuality. National leaders were wanting; Gideon, Jepthah and Samson were only a memory and tradition. Freedom was lost, racial pride and patriotic spirit had vanished, and their vision had faded out. The heroes were gone, the priests had failed, and the prophets had not yet come. Old Eli, the high priest, was a respectable weakling who was swayed by his degenerate sons.

It was a dull, drear, drab sort of time; ideals were low; manhood was flabby and cowardly; all Israel was corrupt and swinishly content. The priestly leaders had allowed morality to decay; there was no promise of any change under the influence of the adulterous Hophni and Phinehas, the degraded offspring of Eli. A revival was sadly needed, but there was no preacher, and worst of all no man out of whom a preacher might be made.

Hannah lived in the hill country of Ephraim, at a little place called Ramathaim-zophim—but who ever heard of Ramathaim-zophim? It was one of the places like the "country God forgot." That name, long, odd and unusual, was the biggest thing about it, and was something to furnish sport for the fellows from the urban parts. But you know that when our cities fail, and the seats of wealth and culture have surrendered, God has a way of finding things at the Ramathaim-zophims of earth. Right at this time, the hope of Israel was at this little out-of-the-way place in the hills of Ephraim. The little community would have remained unhonored and unsung, but for the fact that Hannah lived there.

Who would have believed that the hope of the Reformation was in the hut of a coal miner, and that God was waiting for a husky lad who was growing up there? The Church had forgotten her great commission, and God was waiting for a man, a little cobbler-preacher, toiling at his bench, that he might live and preach on his meager stipend. God waited for Luther and Carey, and so back in those dim days when Hannah prayed at Shiloh for a son, we find God waiting for a man. Think of it! God waiting for a man, and up there in the hill country of Ephraim a poor, disappointed woman praying!

Hannah, the wife of Elkanah, had been denied the crowning glory of the Hebrew woman, the privilege of motherhood. Hannah was just a poor, sad-hearted, simple-souled woman who told her troubles to God; she had prayed a long time for a son, and when she had no child to go with her on their annual visit to Shiloh for worship, her disappointment seemed more than she could bear. On this visit, she became more persistent in her praying. We may learn something by listening in on that prayer, "O LORD of hosts, if thou wilt indeed look on the affliction of thine handmaid, and remember me, and not forget thine handmaid, but wilt give unto thine handmaid a man child, then will I give him unto the LORD all the days of his life, and there shall no razor come upon his head" (I Sam. 1:11).

God Wanted a Man

Here was what God had been waiting for; He wanted a man, but before He could have such a man as He needed, He must have a mother like Hannah. Here lies the glory of the human home; even God could not carry out his plans without the help of that little home in the hills. When God listened to that prayer and that vow, it is as if He said, "I have found a mother and I shall have my man."

It was a sad commentary upon the worship at the tabernacle that old Eli should think that the praying woman was drunk. It reveals the fact that drunkenness was more common than prayer at the services where Eli presided. Nothing more fully sets forth the moral degredation of the nation than that brief colloquy between Eli and Hannah, and it was much more creditable to the poor woman than to the mitered priest.

God passed by the homes of the priest, the mansions of the rich, and stopped at the little home in the hills to hear a woman pray. Hannah was not looking for what people call a career; she was old-fashioned in her thinking, and counted it more important to rear a boy for God than to attain some sort of notoriety outside her home. Hannah believed that being a mother was the most wonderful thing that could come to a woman. A lot of the intelligentsia would not agree with her, but the verdict of history is on her side. No one will know "until the gates of the judgment day unfold" what the world owes to its Hannahs.

Just a plain, country woman! A hill-country woman, if

you please! She had little or no educational advantages; she would have cut a rather sorry figure at most social functions; she was not an expert dancer; she would have been a poor partner at a bridge party; her gowns would hardly have been approved by the taste of the elite; but she was in business with God Almighty. No doubt she was ignored by the society women of her day, but we do not know the name of a single social leader of that period. They had them, of course, and they strutted and strove to surpass each other in the affairs which they gave and the jewels they wore, but the historian saw no reason to write about them; they left no contribution to the world worth recording.

Some people will trade their scanty hope of heaven for one little dish of the cheap pottage of social distinction, which will turn to bitterness under their tongues. They will barter everything worthwhile for the tawdry trappings of a false celebrity, and then find the foibles they obtained are not able to give them real fame or true happiness.

Hannah's name was not on the roster of the four hundred; she was not mentioned as the woman whose gown was one of the attractions of the charity ball, but she somehow got on the honor roll of heaven in the foremost files of eternity. She belonged to the same school as Cornelia, that Roman matron, who thought her splendid boys more rare and valuable than bracelets of gold, clusters of diamonds, or ropes of pearls. Hannah was a praying mother. She did not get very much recognition upon earth, but she had the right of way in heaven's inner circle; and the King put out a busy sign for the angels, when Hannah wanted to talk with Him.

A Mother's Sacrifice

It is interesting to imagine Hannah getting her boy ready to leave home, for the only way that she knew to keep that promise was to take him to Shiloh and leave him there at the place of offering. She had counted the years, the months, the weeks, the days, and then the hours. It was not easy to carry out that vow, for Hannah loved her boy with the passionate ardor of any other mother. Her heart throbbed and ached and then hurt more sorely, as the hour came to carry out that holy covenant. Hannah was of the stuff of which martyrs are made, so at any cost she would keep her word to Jehovah. Let us imagine her getting together that scanty wardrobe—not much at best—out of her poverty. How she wondered who would look after his childish wants, or care for him if he got sick! We know how a mother thinks of all those things.

At last the hour came for the annual trip to Shiloh, and Hannah set out with her boy for the sanctuary. She had not slept much the night before; she had prayed and wrestled with God all night. Time and time again, she had risen from that humble bed and looked at that sleeping face, so chubby and rosy in the dim light of the lamp. If we listen, we can hear the drip of the scalding tears as they fall upon his pillow. Let us think of that journey to Shiloh with little Samuel prattling and lisping his baby words, while every sparkle of his eyes made the task all the harder.

At last, they came to the door of the tent of meeting; the story was soon told and the little fellow taken in charge by one of the Levitical attendants. The little bundle of clothes, every thread woven and stitched by a mother's loving fingers, was handed in; there was one last, clinging embrace, and Hannah turned her feet to the lonely road that led to the little home in the hill country.

What an event! Sacrifices like that are written in gold on the ledgers of heaven. Hannah had given her boy to God—not to business, not to his country, not to the giddy whirl of social gaiety—but to God! Hannah had woven her very heart strings into the warp and woof of those little clothes. Such a mother is worth a million of those whose ambition is to have their children popular with the folk who lead the fashionable set of their day.

Earth knows no more consummate folly than that of the weak, Christian mother who is more anxious to win the patronage of the folk who do not really count than to be true to God. Can anyone think of Hannah asking Eli if he did not think it would be all right for her boy to attend the dances and play cards just for sport? It would be impossible for one to think of Hannah's being concerned about those things; her faith was too deep and genuine. There are a lot of poor simpletons in our churches who talk about allowing their children privileges, when they mean letting them dabble in questionable amusements which weaken spiritual life and unfit them for the highest and holiest.

There is a company of so-called Christian mothers who do not want their children to belong wholly to God. They are teaching them to play with fire, and trying to see how near they can come to the flames and not be burned. Hannah did not have to get into the forbidden pastures to have a good time. The folks who during the Exodus lamented about the onions, the garlic, the leeks, and the cucumbers of Egypt, also loathed the light manna. The praying mothers of the land are not those who sit up at night to make ballroom dresses for girls who have forgotten the way to the prayer meeting.

Boys With Praying Mothers

It will do our hearts good to think of Hannah up there at Ramathaim-zophim and her little boy down there at Shiloh. As time counts, the distance was greater than from New

York to Liverpool with us. Our hearts will feel for that lonely mother, dreaming about the little lad who might be crying himself to sleep in the dark and wondering in his childish way where his mother was. Hannah is to be envied alongside that mother living in a land of schools and churches whose children never hear her pray, and who is not willing to break with the frivolities of life to give them to God and His cause. There is many a mother, sleeping in the same home with her children every night, who is farther from them than Hannah was from Samuel. Her prayers made a golden highway from Ramathaim-zophim to the throne of God, and thence to that little bed where a little boy lay in one of the rooms of the tabernacle. How she wove a protecting armour of faith about that tiny cot, and the angels of the heavenly host encamped about it all night long!

The Lord God of Israel heard a mother who prayed and gave after that sort. By every law of prayer that God has made, by all that He is, by the everlasting faithfulness of His nature, He must hear that sort of praying! Some of us who have compromised with the world and clamored for the things of the flesh have locked the doors of heaven in the face of all the prayers we may offer and thrown away the key. We will want God badly some of these days, but He will be silent and all heaven seem deaf to our cries. It will not be because God is angry, but for the reason that He could not be the God that He is and hear such praying.

One Hannah, lonely woman of the hills, who has given her boy wholly to God, will mean more in the realm of things that endure than ten thousand pleasure-loving women with their names upon the rolls of our churches, whose children would wonder what they were doing should they find them upon their knees. It is the Hannahs of earth who give prophets and leaders to God's Israel; and when a church has had many years to pass and there are no Samuels hearing the voice of God in the stillness of the night, you may be sure that it is lacking in Hannahs who dedicate their children to God before they are born.

The little coat which Hannah carried each year to Shiloh was woven from the very fiber of her soul, every filament hallowed by intercession and stained by the tears of a deathless love. No wonder God called Samuel! He could use the son of Hannah; he was a blade tempered for the fingers of the King. A great preacher, whose voice has rung throughout the world like a silver trumpet, used to tell that on the day he was ordained to the ministry his mother said to him, "Son, I have not spoken to you lest I might unduly influence your mind, but every day since the day you were born I have prayed God that you might be His minister to preach His glorious gospel." Can we wonder that his life has been felt in world-girdling power? Some day, God will have in heaven a memorial for the Hannahs of earth. Their work is too great, too valuable and enduring not to be commemorated.

Hard by the nation's capitol stands the memorial to Abraham Lincoln, the great emancipator, the lonely, tragic figure of the long days of civil strife. It is the nation's tribute to the gaunt, sorrowful, yet mighty man who guided the Union through the maelstrom of that titanic war. But heaven's testimonials will be more durable and beautiful than one built from flinty granite or gleaming bronze. It will be adorned with the gold of sacrificial prayers and gemmed with the lustre of countless tears, transmuted by the alchemy of heaven into jewels fairer than ever gleamed in any earthly diadem, and whiter than the pearls of the southern seas. There it will remain to tell the story of toil, love and sacrifice, till the eternities grow gray with the passing millenniums.

God won Israel back when He found Samuel, and God always finds Samuels in the homes of mothers like Hannah. Hannah was unlearned, save in the lore of the heart. Her training was in that hidden school where the secret of the Lord is revealed to them that fear Him. Yet the mighty years of the kingdom that came after were due in part to this wonderful mother from the hills.

Here we have a mother who succeeded in earth's holiest undertaking, that of consecrated motherhood. To give a son like Samuel to God and humanity was a work that angels might envy. Without Samuel, Israel must have waited long for a ruler like David, or a builder like Solomon. This praying mother filled a beautiful and vital place in the nation's life, and the little home in the hill country of Ephraim was the arena of achievement for a mother who succeeded.

References: I Samuel 1:1–22; 2:1–21; 3:1–21.

Jeroboam

THE MAN WHO LOST HIS CHANCE

THERE are two things which put the acid test to any character—crushing adversity, or sudden success. Prosperity, however, is a more thorough assay than misfortune. What a man does when greatness is thrust upon him reveals, as nothing else, the real fiber of his soul!

No character in the Bible had lofty position given him more abruptly, and none other failed so completely as Jeroboam, the son of Nebat. The remarkable thing about his case was that he was utterly unconscious of his default. When a man fails in business, it is at once known to every one—his friends, his creditors and himself. A man may fail morally, and neither he nor his friends are aware of the catastrophe. Moral failure may not alter his habits of life, as far as outward appearances go. He may live in as good a house, wear as fine clothes, and spend as much money as ever. It takes time to reveal the extent and hurt of inner failure. It was so with Jeroboam; it took long years for the summer of time to ripen his acts, and expose the abject ruin of his moral collapse.

Jeroboam was a young man of great promise. King Solomon, who was a keen judge of men, gave him a place of trust and responsibility. He was in charge of the house of Joseph when the message came from the man of God that changed the whole tenor of his life. Solomon had succumbed at the zenith of his glory. Skilled in all that pertained to statecraft, profound in his worldly wisdom, rich beyond computation, he had fallen pitifully. The golden age of Israel, when silver was counted of little value, was waning, and the sun of the brilliant king was setting behind the clouds of his own sins. Almost like the eclipse of the sun was the dimming of that regal life—the fading of that matchless genius. Pride, lust and idolatry had eroded the structure of that unrivaled mind, and soiled the splendor of that royal soul. His talents and wealth were not dedicated to God.

The prophet told Jeroboam of the fall of Solomon and the trust which Jehovah would place in his hands. If he had been great enough to wait and learn the things which a king ought to know, the story might have been far different. But Jeroboam was unwilling to wait God's time. In some way, he challenged the authority of the king, and had to flee for his life. He went into Egypt where he schemed and plotted until Solomon was dead. When the scepter fell from his lifeless hand, the rising tide of discontent burst forth; the malcontents needed a leader and sent for Jeroboam.

The record says that Jeroboam was "a mighty man of valor." Evidently, this meant more than mere physical courage, and is intended to mean that this man possessed many of the qualities of leadership. Folk don't send for weaklings when they prepare to challenge kings. Jeroboam came; his hour had struck, and he felt himself the child of destiny. He did not come to reconcile Israel with Rehoboam; he came to seize a throne and establish a dynasty. Rehoboam, the foolish son of a wise father, threw away his opportunity to hold his throne and become a successful ruler. Jeroboam knew something of what the answer would be when they proposed to the young king retrenchment in government expenses and lowering of taxes, even before it was announced. He was too astute a politician to offer terms which the son of Solomon would accept.

The Folly of Rehoboam

Rehoboam, like the fabled donkey, tried to don the lion's skin and roar loud enough to terrify the rebels, but the people were too much in earnest to be easily frightened. The heavy taxes in time and money which had been collected to build the magnificent temple, the sumptuous palace and the numerous cities which adorned the land had exhausted them. The people were set upon economy and would not be denied. When the young king made his foolish and bullying answer, Jeroboam seized the opportunity. The ancient cry of the nation, "To your tents, O Israel," was raised, and the hated tax collector was stoned. Rehoboam fled to Jerusalem, and the ten tribes called for Jeroboam and made him king.

The man had now reached the goal of his ambition; Jehovah had fulfilled His word, and the exile was now upon a throne. The son of the widow of Ephrath, whom the genius of David and the munificence of Solomon had made famous, was now ruler of a people.

Then Jeroboam came to his first real test. He had come to greatness and power, almost unsought and unachieved, and now he must measure up to his task or fail. Know what a man will do in the high noon of his success and the midnight of his adversity, and you have the full measure of his manhood. It is not given to many men to know when they are making the decisions which build them or destroy them. The choices that shape the future are often about seemingly little things, apart from the great currents of life.

Thus far Jeroboam had succeeded according to the word of the prophet. The ten tribes and the greater part of the territory were his. All that had happened, the revolt of the people and the choice of Jehovah, had called for little effort on his part, but now it became necessary to shape national policies. In the past, the life of Israel had been built about their religion; and success or failure had depended upon their loyalty to Jehovah. God had made Jeroboam king, and it remained to be seen how the new ruler would act toward Jehovah. Events soon proved that he was more anxious to guard his throne than to build the moral life of his people. He fondly assumed that he was too occupied with big things to give much time or consideration to the God who had made him king.

He was at once confronted with a problem of statecraft which was pivotal in his career and the life of his new nation. All Israel had been going up, at least once each year, to worship at the resplendent temple which had become the center of their religious life. This annual pilgrimage had become the great event of the year to most of them. Jeroboam and his advisers felt that if this continued, the ten tribes would, sooner or later, renew their allegiance to the house of David. Here was the great problem: the people were going to worship, yet they must not go back to Jerusalem. This was the first real test for the new king. Jehovah had said, "And it shall be, that if thou wilt hearken to all that I command thee, and wilt walk in my ways, and do that is right in my sight, to keep my statutes and commandments, as David my servant did; that I will be with thee, and build thee a sure house, as I built for David, and will give Israel unto thee" (I Kings 11:38).

The Folly of Forsaking God

Most of God's promises of earthly greatness have conditions, and so in this promise to Jeroboam, but the new king forgot that. The question that confronted him was, Would he follow the word of Jehovah, and trust and obey Him; or would he listen to the voice of worldly wisdom, and rule as the princes without God were accustomed to do? Jeroboam decided that the wisest thing to do was to get rid of Jehovah; too much religion was an impediment to a fellow who was going to be a great king. Doubtless, he reasoned after this fashion: "The best thing to do will be to change the object of worship; for as long as the people worship Jehovah they will want to go to the temple, and that will mean they will return to the house of David and I will lose my crown."

So Jeroboam traded the support of Jehovah for a policy which he thought would make his throne secure. Jehovah had given him the throne and would have kept His word, but Jeroboam did not think that he needed Him very much since he had gotten the kingdom. The golden calves were a political expedient; they were supposed to represent the creative power of Jehovah; but in reality they led the people back to the bestial idolatry of Egypt.

The politicians doubtless thought that the new king had done a very shrewd thing and showed himself a master diplomat. A man going wrong, especially if that man is a king, has plenty of fawning admirers to tell him how wonderful he is. One of these calves was set up in the extreme northern part of the kingdom, that the people there might have a place of worship and feel free from the long journey to Jerusalem. The other was placed in the southern part on the great highway that led to Jerusalem, where everyone that went that way would see it.

The plan worked, as far as the people's going to Jerusalem was concerned; but the result was quite different from what Jeroboam had planned. Instead of securing his throne, it determined the end of his line. The Bible is very plain about the works of Jeroboam: fourteen times we read of the kings that followed him, "And he walked in the way of Jeroboam the son of Nebat, who made Israel to sin." "Made Israel to sin!" The whole nation was corrupted through the works of this man; the people followed their new king in the downward path.

What a record it was! The sins of Jeroboam became a model; his was the sign board which pointed down the road that led away from the God of their fathers. Jeroboam was the marker, standing where the broad thoroughfare of iniquity left the straight way of the law of Moses. He blazed out the trail, until it was named for him:—"The way of Jeroboam the son of Nebat." A man who could so lead a people astray might have kept them true to the covenant they had made, but he was not big enough to risk all with God.

What Was the Sin of Jeroboam?

It was not a life of vice; there is no intimation that he lived a debauched life, or that he was personally vicious. It was the sin of selling out for political advantage; it was trading Jehovah for what he thought was a stable throne. He decided he was a great statesman, and, like his modern imitators, he did not believe in mixing politics with religion. He was not going to be irreligious, but he was going to have two compartments in his life; one where God might have a place, and another where he would play politics to save his throne. He knew that God had rejected Solomon and that he owed his place to the will of Jehovah, yet his love of power and his desire to hold his position by his own shrewdness led him to this fatal blunder.

Poor Jeroboam never knew how signally he had failed; he lived and died a king, but from that hour of decision, he and his line were doomed. He sold out his one great opportunity and sold it cheap. He listened to the siren voice of worldly ambition, and turned to the left. His monuments were the golden calves, the deserted altars of Jehovah, and the ruin of a nation that followed its king. It is a tragically pitiful spectacle to see a man of unusual powers fail just when the tides of fortune have set in his favor.

It is the fate of some men to be remembered by their blunders and delinquencies. Grouchy was one of the brilliant cluster of marshals that surrounded the mighty Napoleon; he had rendered gallant service on many stricken fields, but the world remembers him as the man who failed his great leader at Waterloo. John Mark had many noble qualities, but the retreat from Perga is more often coupled with his name than the Gospel which he wrote. The world forgets very slowly the failure of the man who had great opportunities. Jeroboam was a mighty man of valor; he had been tested in battle strife, but no one has written the story of his valiant deeds. The one thing pre-eminent in his record is that he caused Israel to sin.

Alfred the Great is known as the founder of England's mighty navy; Alexander Hamilton, as the man who set the feet of our infant republic on the road to financial greatness; Louis Pasteur, as the discoverer who opened new doors to the progress of the healing forces of the world. Jeroboam, the valiant, the virile, the founder of a new dynasty, is remembered for the evil which he did. He was the leader of a host which followed its chieftain to disgrace and ruin, a man loved and honored who deceived his followers into irretrievable blunders. Such was the fate of a man who allowed his selfish policy and unholy ambition to hold the scales of destiny in a pivotal hour.

"Jeroboam the son of Nebat, who made Israel to sin." Listen to the dull heavy tones of that epitaph and you hear the deep dirge of the bells of doom. What did he do? What is his story? "He made." Made what? "Made Israel to sin."

See the spectral line: men with hoary heads, women stooped
and bent, strong men, mature women, flaming youth, prattling children, all of them turned away from God by this
man. Who is he? Yonder he goes at the head of the column
—strong, ambitious, plausible and fascinating! It is Jeroboam,
the son of Nebat, "who made Israel to sin." That is his
position in the light of history; the first of that long line of
evil men who ruled the northern kingdom of Israel. When
the inspired writer began to tell this story, he wrote, "A
mighty man of valor," for he found no more fitting words
to describe this stalwart young man. When his work was
finished, the same historian looked over the land sodden with
idolatry and wandering away from God, heaved a sigh and
wrote, dipping his pen into the blackest ink and blurring it
meanwhile with his tears, "Jeroboam the son of Nebat, who
made Israel to sin."

The Results of Infidelity

Voltaire gave the keenest wit, the greatest display of satire in
that brilliant age to which he belonged, when he attempted
to jibe religion off of the earth. A nation walked in his
teachings until their land was drenched with tears and blood.
The French revolution with its prisons and guillotines was the
fruitage of the work of men like him. Long after Jeroboam
was gone, when none of his line sat upon the throne, the
impetus which he gave to those forces was felt. No other
king needed to find the pathway to doom, for Jeroboam had
marked it out. He established a new kingdom, but he turned
his feet toward the places where the beastly gods of Egypt
held sway and the fires of Moloch burned. The nation followed his leading into the deadly paralyzing sins which
brought their destruction.

The Spirit-guided penman looked over the ruin and picked up his quill. How slowly he wrote! "Jeroboam the son of Nebat"—and then he paused, wondering how to finish the story. The Holy Spirit whispered, "Behold his works"; then grasping his pen a little more firmly, he finished the sentence, writing just a little heavier line, *"who made Israel to sin,"* and closed the book.

References: I Kings, chapters 11 to 16; II Chronicles, chapters 10 to 13.

Jonah

THE PREACHER WHO DID NOT WANT
TO SUCCEED

THOSE who think that God showed no consideration for
the great Gentile world before the coming of Christ will
have to explain the work of Jonah, for all his recorded work
was outside the land of Israel. Had it not been for his call
to preach to a heathen city and his running away from it, we
would have known little or nothing of him.

Jonah was sent out of Israel when it seemed there was every
reason for his being kept at home. The nation was in the
darkest days in all its history and hastening to its doom, yet its
leading prophet was sent to carry God's message into the heart
of heathendom. To say that there are lots of heathen in the
homeland is no Biblical reason for neglecting the lost who
know not the way of life.

Jonah lived in the northern kingdom in the time of
Jeroboam II. He was a patriotic Hebrew who wanted to see
his nation kept as the favored of God. He was astute enough
to see the danger in the growing Assyrian empire and wanted
to see it broken up. He saw that if they continued their
conquests that Israel would lose its independence and become
simply an Assyrian province.

When God called him to carry His word to Nineveh, he
did not want to go. Jonah did not want to see Nineveh
repent; he fully believed that if they did repent, Jehovah in
His mercy would spare them; he wanted them destroyed that
they might no longer be a menace to his people. He failed

to understand that the best way to protect themselves from Assyria was to bring them to know God and His holy law. Jonah was like some modern church members whose patriotism and racial prejudices are stronger than their care for the command of God and the souls of men. The world still needs very badly to learn the lesson taught in the book of Jonah.

Moved by these motives, Jonah tried to evade the call of the Lord and took ship for Tarshish. Tarshish was the furtherest point west that the Hebrew world knew anything about. Jonah was going in the opposite direction to Nineveh and going as far as he could. Doubtless, he thought that if he could get that far from his duty that somehow God would forget him and not trouble him any more. Some preachers shirk from fear of failure, but Jonah was afraid of success. His attitude can only be explained in the light of his intense nationalism and Jewish prejudice. Rather than see the Ninevehites converted and spared, he would not preach to them at all, and sought to get as far from the hated city as possible.

Running Away From God Is Perilous

Jonah was not the last preacher who tried to run away from his God-given task and got into trouble. The man who tries to run away from God has set out upon a long and perilous journey, for God has a way of dealing with runaway preachers, as this one found out to his sorrow. The Lord sent a mighty storm and the little bark which held the truant preacher was in mighty peril. It seems strange that Jonah was the only man on the ship who could sleep during the terrible storm, but a backslider is usually the most unconcerned person in the community; until the Holy Spirit begins to trouble him, his conscience is deadened and he seems content in his sin.

Jonah was glad to be so far from Nineveh, and yet the Lord was just beginning to deal with him; he was going to be mighty sorry, but he could sleep all right for the time being. When he was aroused by the frightened sailors, Jonah knew at once that God was after him and that he had not escaped. To his credit it may be said that he did not lie about it, and was willing to pay the penalty for his disobedience. God, however, did not want Jonah to die; He wanted him to preach in Nineveh and meant to see that he did what He had told him. There are times when the fellow who has run away from duty had rather die than face God.

Many things, most of them foolish, have been said about Jonah and the whale, yet the word "whale" is not in the book. The record says that God had prepared a "great fish" to discipline the recreant prophet, and He had no trouble making one big enough for His purpose. Jonah was swallowed by the fish which God had prepared, and spent three days and nights in that strange environment. We might wish that we knew more about that unusual experience of the prophet, but many things we might wish to know are not told us. One very successful but illiterate evangelist used to say that Jonah took a degree from "Whale College." Whatever we may think about the event, Jonah learned some things down there that the colleges do not teach. He learned to pray very earnestly, something which he had not done since he decided to run away, and that is a mighty good lesson for any preacher. When Jonah cried to God from those crowded and uncomfortable quarters, he was making more progress in all that a preacher ought to know than when he was running toward Joppa to catch that ship.

He learned some good theology in this most unique school. He found out that "they that observe lying vanities forsake their own mercy." He once fondly thought that he could run away from God. The devil will tell any preacher who thinks after this fashion just how very up to date he is, and how his theories are confirmed by the discoveries of modern science, but Jonah learned better. He learned that the man who forsakes the fountain of the everlasting mercies and tries to get away from duty is following "lying vanities." So long as a man obeys God, God is responsible for the way in which things come out; but the fellow who will not go God's way must meet and solve all the problems by himself, and does not often get the correct answer. Jonah was down there in the belly of the fish because he had forsaken the mercies of God and had listened to lies which were worse than vanity.

Another wonderful discovery was the cry, "Salvation is of the Lord." There are quite a lot of so-called preachers in the world who could profitably spend a whole semester in "Whale College," if only they might learn this one thing. Jonah learned his lesson in the school of chastisement which was very painful. The tuition rate was high, but he never forgot the lesson! We commend the school which Jonah attended to all those who think that salvation is of human effort rather than sovereign grace. They would be more humbled and would look a little bedraggled when they received their diplomas, but their theology would be straighter and their sermons would get better results.

Better Learn to Obey God

Jonah learned to obey God down there. When he found himself once more on dry land, he looked at the sun and set his course for Nineveh. He had learned that disobedience brings trouble, and when God said, "Preach unto them the preaching that I bid thee," he did not try to edit the message. There was not much originality in his preaching, and not much chance for display of scholarship, but there was power!

When a man does just what God tells him, he does not have to worry about what is going to happen. That is God's business! If the fellows who prate about the book of Jonah being a myth would learn just this one thing from the book, much of their preaching would be transformed and the number of converts increased in like ratio. The fellow is assuming a fearful responsibility who assumes to improve upon the message given him by God Almighty.

Jonah's preaching was not what some folks would call popular. It was a declaration of coming judgment, just the sort of thing some people would call crude and heartless, but it stirred Nineveh. That revival was possibly one of the most spectacular in all history, for all the city came to the mourner's bench. The account says that they humbled themselves and cried mightily unto God. Some folks don't like sackcloth and ashes and are made nervous by loud praying. All of those things were at Nineveh, and Jesus spoke approvingly of their repentance. It was no dry-eyed, cold-blooded revival that Jonah held in Nineveh.

The fact is that every great spiritual awakening in history has had some things which the more shallow-minded and fastidious do not like. They always cry out about fanatacism and excitement, but sin, judgment, heaven and hell are big subjects; and when people think deeply about them they are likely to feel just as deeply as they think. Sackcloth and ashes do not appeal to the more meticulous and over-cautious, but when people are dealing with things of life and death they will forget some of the formal proprieties. We should be very careful lest in trying to get rid of the sackcloth and the ashes we leave out the repentance and the praying. Jesus was a better judge of what constitutes repentance than some of our modern critics.

Yes, Nineveh repented and was spared. God has ever kept

an open door for the folk who repent, and Nineveh found His everlasting mercy, which was the last thing Jonah wanted to see come to them. Jonah hoped that Nineveh would not repent; he wanted to see the judgment of God upon them. He built a booth upon a hill overlooking the city from the east and waited the forty days. He was greatly disappointed when the mercy of God spared the city. God tried by the fate of the sheltering gourd-vine to teach him and all other men that His plans are bigger than Israel, and that divine love and grace have no national boundaries. We are touched by the tender words which speak of the sixscore thousand innocents who would suffer, as well as the helpless cattle. God did not want to cause needless suffering to any of His creatures, and the unsinning animals were also in the mind of the Father.

Lessons to Be Studied Today

The lessons of the book of Jonah are needed today. God's mercy is for all men, and His love embraces all colors, races and nationalities. This day needs this lesson as well as those in the time of Jonah. Every anti-missionary ought to memorize this book.

A man does not get away from God by running away, however far or fast he may go. God was just as near Tarshish as He was to Joppa, and while Jonah might have been farther from Nineveh, he was no further from the God who told him to go there. Jonah was not the last man who has tried to run away from Omnipresence and learned the folly of it. God knows just where Tarshish is and the way there much better than we do.

The preacher who will do just what God tells him will not be held accountable for success or failure; in fact, the one who obeys God has already succeeded. The message of Jonah was the undiluted word of the Lord; it was not emasculated nor toned down, and God took care of it. The Almighty is abundantly able to look after His word, and it needs no human redactor to make it effective. This explains the marked success of some men who have had little training and educational endowment. Far better faithful men with God than university degrees without the divine anointing.

Real revivals will have some outward manifestations; there will be sorrow and tears, and sometimes sackcloth and ashes; and convicted folk will not be ashamed of their praying. Just as long as men and women are more concerned about what the onlookers may think than about the mercy of God, a revival will not reach places like Nineveh. True repentance means amendment of life, and where men do not turn from the evil that is in their hands God will pay little attention. Nineveh, crying mightily unto Him with sackcloth and ashes, looked better to the Almighty than Nineveh dressed up, going on in sin.

We are not told how fully Jonah came to see and rejoice in God's universal mercy, but we may hope that he came to see the truth and became a better man. God has no perfect men to use, so He uses the tools that are best to His hand and tries to improve them as He uses them. Jonah was the best man God could find to hold a revival in Nineveh and He used him. When we see our own faults and weaknesses, we wonder that God uses us at all, and then we realize anew that this treasure is still in earthen vessels.

The reason for the wonderful results of Jonah's preaching lies in the fact that Jonah did just what the Lord told him. When human wisdom and worldly motives undertake to revise the message and make it more palatable, we have to depend upon ourselves and it is ineffective. If we of today will preach "the preaching" He bids us, there will be some modern Ninevehs in sackcloth and ashes crying for mercy un-ashamed.

Jonah made some ugly mistakes, but he has learned better in heaven; and a great many other preachers will have a lot to learn when they get to that place where we see the Lord Jesus face to face and know as we are known. Some of us will have to start mighty close to the foot of the class, but it is good to know that we will have plenty of time, true text-books, and a Teacher who makes no blunders.

References: II Kings 14:25; Jonah, entire book.

Ahab

WEAK BUT WICKED

WHEN Ahab became the ruler of the northern kingdom of Israel, he set a new standard in the scale of kingly depravity. He moved the hands on the dial of the register of wickedness farther than any one among their monarchs— and several of them were not amateurs in sin.

The record says of him, "And Ahab the son of Omri did evil in the sight of the LORD above all that were before him. And it came to pass, as if it had been a light thing for him to walk in the sins of Jeroboam the son of Nebat, that he took to wife Jezebel the daughter of Ethbaal king of the Zidonians, and went and served Baal, and worshipped him. . . . And Ahab made a grove; and Ahab did more to provoke the LORD God of Israel to anger than all the kings of Israel that were before him" (I Kings 16:30–33).

This is what the inspired record says of Ahab. His father Omri had surpassed all his predecessors in wickedness, and if Ahab had not come along he might have held the belt for kingly deviltry. It is a wonderful thing to start a line upward, but when bad fathers are followed by worse sons, things are indeed on the down grade.

Marriage either makes or mars a man, and when the woman is the stronger character, it makes a thorough job one way or the other. Ahab married Jezebel, and that says more than it sounds, for Jezebel was a woman who made things happen, and none of them were good things. A weak and vicious man, with a strong wife who is worse than he is, makes a combination which pleases his satanic majesty.

It was a dark day for Israel when this degenerate weakling came to the throne, and a still more gloomy one when he brought the cruel, capable and idolatrous daughter of Zidon to share his rule. Some men are noted for one thing and some for another, but Ahab's sole claim to pre-eminence came from his outstanding sins. Israel had known idolatry before he came to the throne, but it was mainly like the golden calves of Jeroboam; however, now there came in a flood of the foul, sensual paganism that had rotted the life of Phoenicia.

History knows no worship which more fully surrendered to all that is base in human nature, and which so completely mingled with their concept of religion the lowest passions of the race. Sexual immorality had been found in the degeneracy of every civilization, but the rites established in Israel under Ahab made vice a part of their religious life. The temples of Baal and the groves of Astarte became centers of vice in the name of piety.

One may judge the moral status of a people when the things which are regarded as holy become unspeakably vile. There is no doubt that Jezebel felt that she was doing what ought to be done. She had been steeped from childhood in that sort of worship in her own land. It was different with Ahab; he knew the place which the worship of Jehovah held in the life of Israel; he knew all about how her traditions and memories—as well as her hopes—clustered about the faith of Abraham and Moses. Ahab knew all this, but under the influence of this beautiful and aggressive woman he used all the power and prestige of his throne to establish the abominations which destroyed the worship of Jehovah and degraded the lives of his people.

Ahab Distinguished for Wickedness

The only distinction Ahab ever enjoyed was in wickedness. Some kings were great soldiers; some were builders of cities; others were skilled in statecraft, but Ahab was paramount in sin. How far he would have gone without Jezebel we do not know, but his inclinations were evil and this dominating woman only led him deeper into the depths of sin.

One must understand the awful things which Ahab and Jezebel were setting up to appreciate the earnestness and vehemence of Elijah. Ahab stood for Baal and debauchery; Elijah was the champion of Jehovah, and of purity in life and worship. The story of their contest is vividly told in the first book of Kings, and the tale of the famine and the victory upon Carmel are among the religious classics of the world.

Ahab knew the will of God, but Jezebel was beautiful and the worship of Baal and Ashtoreth called for no self-denial. Their rituals were gorgeous and voluptuous, and the things which they allowed were pleasing to the flesh; so Ahab went with the tide. The abominations of their secret ceremonies were agreeable to his weak and sensuous nature, so he gave all that he had for Baal and against Jehovah. It is a sin to be weak and vacillating, when all that is worth-while is at stake and mighty issues hang in the balances.

Some men are weak while wanting to be good, but Ahab was weak and striving to be bad. Jezebel was not weak; she was strong to do evil. She knew what she wanted; she wanted the religion of her native land to supplant the faith of Jehovah, and she sought with all her power to bring it about. Ahab lacked character and decision, but he went headlong for all that Jezebel wanted.

The struggle between Elijah and Ahab came to a climax when the priests of Baal accepted the challenge of the answer by fire. Ahab was mightily impressed by the miracle of

Carmel; he knew that Elijah was right and that Jehovah had answered. It is entirely possible that he joined in the shout, "Jehovah, he is the God"; but when he got back to Jezreel and looked into the face of Jezebel and felt her entwining arms, he consented to her plan to murder the prophet. If Ahab had been strong enough to stand for that which he knew was right, Israel might have been brought back to the worship of Jehovah, but he was lacking in moral fiber and cared little for the glory or the doom of the nation. To live in ease, to gratify his whims and passions, to bask in the smiles of Jezebel, these were the big things of life to him; so he plunged anew into his sinful course.

Ahab Covets Naboth's Vineyard

A vivid exhibition of the flaccidity of Ahab and the heartless domination of Jezebel is found in the story of Naboth and his vineyard. The land of this good man joined hard upon the grounds of the palace and Ahab wanted his beautiful vineyard for an additional garden. Following the immemorial custom of the Hebrews, Naboth refused to sell his family inheritance. Ahab went home sulking like a spoiled moron; he turned his face to the wall and pouted, refusing even to eat. His conduct was more like that of some wilful child than that of the ruler of a nation.

On this occasion the cruel and conscienceless nature of Jezebel flared up. Listen to her coarse, sarcastic words to this impotent husband, "Dost thou now govern the kingdom of Israel? Arise, and eat bread, and let thine heart be merry; I will give thee the vineyard of Naboth the Jezreelite" (I Kings 21:7). How full these words were of contempt for her feeble, pusillanimous husband, as well as the utmost disregard for justice and right! In a little while, under the direction of Jezebel, Naboth was condemned and executed under an old statute for which neither king nor queen cared one iota. He was accused of blaspheming God and the king. Jezebel cared nothing for the name of Jehovah and had mighty little respect for that of the king; she hated the one and despised the other. Unscrupulous rulers often become sticklers for law and justice when they have some wicked scheme to carry out. The plot was diabolically hypocritical, but it got rid of Naboth, and that was the object in view.

Naboth was dead, and the king who should have been the protector of his people went down to seize his vineyard as the estate of a condemned felon. One cannot keep back the feeling of indignation and contempt for such actions upon the part of those in authority.

Down there at the vineyard he met Elijah. Thank God for the Elijahs all along the years who have met guilty men in the hours of their seeming triumphs! Ahab trembled before the fearless old prophet and there was both fear and hate in the petulant whine, "Hast thou found me, O mine enemy?" The unrepentant sinner always looks upon the man who reproves him of sin as his enemy. Elijah would have been the best friend Ahab had in all Israel if he would have allowed him to be. The worst foes of Ahab were his vile associates and his sins, but like many others he could not see things as they were.

Ahab Guilty of Murder

The words of the prophet were terse and stern; he charged Ahab with murder and robbery, with killing and taking possession. One hardly knows which to wonder at most, the courage and fidelity of Elijah or the craven weakness of Ahab. The relentless Elijah foretold the doom of his house, and told him that the scavenger dogs would lick his blood where Naboth had died, and devour the body of Jezebel under the walls of Jezreel. The flaccid Ahab cowered before the dread sentence and for the only time in his life showed signs of real penitence. Because of his seeming contrition, the sentence of Jehovah against his house was postponed till after his death; but pay day came and the howling mongrels licked his blood on the chariot that bore his slaughtered body from the fateful field of Ramoth-Gilead, and gnawed the bones of Jezebel after she had been trodden under the hoofs of the steeds of Jehu. Kings and queens are not exempt from the day when inexorable justice pays off, and retribution is no respecter of persons.

Ahab was not strong enough to repent, for repentance is manful work. Ahab could be sorry, but being sorry is not all there is to this thing which God calls repentance. He was not big enough nor brave enough to break with the ways of Jezebel, nor to withstand her imperious will. Strong men, when convinced of the vileness and ruin of sin, turn from their wicked ways unto God and are forgiven; while weaklings, caught in the current of their passions, are helpless against their environment, and are often swept on to their doom. It is possible that apart from Jezebel Ahab might have been brought back to Jehovah, but he lacked the strength to resist the wiles and iron will of this remarkable woman. His country went from bad to worse under his leadership and hastened to its impending fall. Elijah seemed to have withdrawn himself from the life of the king, whose reformation was hopeless, and after the scene at the vineyard of Naboth, he met him no more.

Ahab lived all his life in a palace, but he was never a real king, and his closing years were shadowed by his coming fate. He wore royal robes but they were no defense from the judgment which the prophet foretold. Someone has said that God's judgments move with "leaden feet," but they strike with "iron hands."

Too weak to be a ruler, poor Ahab was great only in his tragic ruin. He was mighty only in wrong doing, eminent in naught save iniquity. He has a place in history because he sat upon a throne, but the depths of his degeneracy destroyed his line. Too weak to be a warrior of renown, too slothful and mediocre of mind for a statesman, he was distinguished like Nero for his cruelty and the debauchery of his nation. He was never able to see the blight which his evil doing had brought, but brazenly sought to blame the reproving prophet. He was born to the purple, but lived only to besmirch it. He inherited a throne, but he made it a curse to the nation and to his posterity. Life opened for him in a palace and ended in gloomy defeat.

The manner of Ahab's death emphasized the power of Jehovah, whom he had sought to dethrone. His place in the record is that of one who surpassed others in vileness, and whose monument was the pile of his sons' heads outside the gates of Jezreel. He was weak and all his weakness was toward evil. He was not weak wanting to be good but he was lacking in decision, and was led headlong into all manner of evil. The judgment of God waited long but it came, and all his sins came in one dire hour to judgment.

> "Though the mills of God grind slowly,
>   Yet they grind exceedingly small;
> Though with patience He stands waiting,
>   With exactness grinds He all."

"And Ahab the son of Omri did evil in the sight of the Lord above all that were before him."

References: I Kings, chapters 16 to 22; II Chronicles 18:1-34.

Manasseh

A MIRACLE OF MERCY

THE sons of good men do not always turn out well. This by no means contradicts the Scriptures about training up a child in the way he should go. There are really good men who make mighty poor fathers. It no more follows that a man is a good father because he is a good man, than being a good man guarantees that one will be a good teacher or a good carpenter. Fatherhood is a serious task and must be worked at with godly intelligence.

Manasseh was the son of Hezekiah, the best of the kings who reigned over the southern kingdom of Judah. He labored mightily for his country, but failed with his boy. It may be that Hezekiah was so busy reforming the nation that he left his boy to others; besides, an eastern harem was a mighty poor place to rear a boy.

At the tender age of twelve, Manasseh was placed upon the throne. The great responsibilities which belonged to that position came to him at the time he should have been in school. There are always evil men and flatterers about a king, and this boy was too young to be proof against their influence. He evidently came under the dominance of some of that group ever present in Jerusalem, who sympathized with the customs of the heathen round about them. From whatever reason he failed, he was weak where it counted most, and broke down where breaking meant ruin.

Manasseh set himself to undo all that his devoted father had accomplished. A roll of his evil deeds reads like the full measure of total depravity. He labored to restore the corrupting idolatry which his father had driven out. The high places where heathendom found shelter were rebuilt, and altars to Baal and Ashtoreth were again erected in the land. Their vile and obscene orgies corrupted the social life of the nation and weakened its moral fiber. He followed the example of the world-ruling Assyrians and introduced the worship of the heavenly bodies. Not only were the sun, the moon, and the stars made objects of worship, but, in daring defiance of Jehovah, he polluted the temple with their altars.

The worship of Baal and Ashtoreth appealed to all that was lowest in human nature, and under the guise of religion led the people into the vilest forms of sensual debauchery. He also introduced the horrid worship of Moloch, with its heartless custom of child sacrifices. Even the son of the king was made to pass through the fire, and this most abhorrent form of paganism was added to the forsaking of Jehovah.

He became infatuated with the low necromancy and witchcraft which were prevalent among the surrounding nations and which were positively forbidden by the law of Moses. He observed the lucky days named by the soothsayers and patronized the infamous wizards who were much like the medicine men of savage countries at the present.

As if to show his complete disregard of all that his fathers held sacred, he desecrated the holy temple with an idol which he had made. The use of images in worship had been forbidden by the second commandment, and the temple was to be bare of anything that would call the mind of the worshiper from the invisible and holy God. In this act there was daring defiance and willful challenge of the holy One of Israel. It was as if he had said, "I am dethroning the God of Abraham, and in His place I am putting another god." Here was the crowning insult of his career, the very wantonness of dare-deviltry, the final step in casting off the God of Israel.

The Most Wicked King of Judah

The record says that Manasseh went beyond the sins of the nations whom God had blotted out to make room for the Hebrews. He seemed to have had an unholy ambition to excel in wickedness, and show how completely he had broken with the holy past of their history. He stands at the head of the class in the worst school of evil-doing which the world has known. He was chief of those who pride themselves on being experts in iniquity. But even now we have not turned all the pages of this life in which black is mingled with crimson. We are told in the story of his reign as recorded in Kings, "Moreover Manasseh shed innocent blood very much, till he had filled Jerusalem from one end to another" (II Kings 21:16). In addition to his sins of idolatry, witchcraft and lust, horrid murder stalked through the holy city, and foul assassinations covered it with the blood of the guiltless. There is a Jewish legend that Isaiah, the golden-mouthed, evangelical prophet, the friend and counsellor of his father, was among the victims.

Let us get a good look at this evil life. Here is a man of the line of David, chosen of God to keep the faith and rule in righteousness, who had betrayed every trust, defied Jehovah and led the nation into foul and bestial idolatry which spread vice like an eating-cancer. He caused the people to forget their God, and defiled his own offspring in the heartless and revolting worship of the malevolent Moloch. He was the pioneer in new forms of iniquity, the explorer of paths of infamy for the feet of the unwary. He used his position to prostitute and betray the divine purpose and holy intent for the chosen nation. Every law was broken with willful intent and impudent challenge. The hands of this man dripped with innocent blood, until the crimson stones of Jerusalem cried to heaven against him. The messengers of God were despised and ignored, and their martyrdom added to this long scroll of moral obliquity. No more repellent character stands out in the long record of sin than that of Manasseh.

Retribution Finally Came

The hosts of the Assyrian once more camped around the walls of Jerusalem, but this time there was no angel of God to "spread his wings on the blast" and protect the doomed city. Jerusalem was taken, and Manasseh was bound in chains and found himself in some cold, damp dungeon of Babylon, where he was left to remember his sins and his fall. Here he had time to meditate upon the evil deeds which had wrought his ruin, and to learn the folly of his course. How that gloomy cell must have thronged with the ghosts of his victims and been filled with the memory of his shame! We can only faintly imagine the bitter remorse of this degraded and humbled king, for Manasseh had not sinned in ignorance; his course had been headstrong and defiant toward God and His law.

How long he was there the record does not say, but it was long enough for him to chew the bitter cud of reflection, and learn that his sins had been above the sins of other men. One might wish that we knew something of the prayers of Manasseh and the pungency of his repentance. We know that no half-way measures satisfied Jehovah, for He was the same God before whom David had poured out his penitence in the heart-wringing words of the Fifty-first Psalm. We are told that "He besought the Lord his God, and humbled himself greatly before the God of his fathers, and prayed unto him: and he was entreated of him, and heard his supplication, and brought him again to Jerusalem into his kingdom" (II Chron. 33:12, 13). Moses had written: "The LORD, The LORD God, merciful and gracious, longsuffering, and abundant in goodness and truth, keeping mercy for thousands, forgiving iniquity and transgression and sin" (Exod. 34:6,7). Manasseh must have felt that his sins tried the limits of these matchless words.

God heard Manasseh! Then surely no other sinner need fear to trust His infinite mercy! Manasseh was forgiven; the long account of his vileness was washed white; the deep crimson stains were made clean; and he who had run before the multitude to do evil found abundant mercy. No wonder that Micah spoke of the God "who delighteth in mercy." This record was left that no man might say, "My guilt is beyond the mercy of God." So long as the story of Manasseh lives upon the sacred page, no one among the sinners of earth need despair.

The repentance of this man was sincere. He came back from Babylon and tried to undo the evil which he had wrought. We read, "And he took away the strange gods, and the idol out of the house of the LORD, and all the altars that he had built in the mount of the house of the LORD, and in Jerusalem, and cast them out of the city. And he repaired the altar of the LORD, and sacrificed thereon peace offerings and thank offerings, and commanded Judah to serve the LORD God of Israel" (II Chron. 33:15,16).

Manasseh found out, however, that it is much easier to sow tares than to root them out. Many of the people who had followed him headlong into the worship of the lecherous and hideous gods which he had established found the ways of license more pleasing to the flesh than the pure religion of

Jehovah with its inflexible laws, and so the high places remained and their evils cursed the land. It is profoundly pitiful to see a man, who has set in motion forces that curse and blight others, trying with tears of remorse to undo the things which he has done and failing in the attempt.

The boy whom the dram-drinker taught to drink does not quit when he does. The youth that learned profanity from his lips will not become reverent when he ceases to swear. The vile seducer may repent, but the victim often lives a life that curses society long after his life has changed.

The Law of Sowing and Reaping

There is an inflexible law of sowing and reaping, which even the pardoning reach of infinite mercy does not revoke. God may and often does forgive the sinner, but that does not destroy the evil influences of a bad life. God has never promised to take away the effects of our sins in other lives; on the contrary, he has told men that their sins shall curse their posterity to the third and fourth generations. In fact, the results of sin cannot be taken away without abrogating the laws of personal responsibility. Long after Manasseh slept with his fathers, the curse of his evil life hung over the land of Judah and Jerusalem; really, it shaded it until the Chaldeans blotted out in blood and smoke the remnant of the glory of David and the splendor of Solomon.

Even this does not end the sad story; the son of the forgiven king did not forget the sins which his father had set before him, and the paths in which they led became pleasant to his feet. Part of the price which Manasseh paid for his years of sin was the ruin of the son who followed him on the throne. When poor, murdered Amon lay cold in death at the close of an evil reign, it was just another item in the account of Manasseh's transgressions. "Sin, when it is full-grown, bringeth forth death," and the death may include others beside the one who sowed the seeds of evil. There are some things which the boundless mercy of God does not take away. God will forgive, but each man must repent for himself, and the son who followed this father's footsteps did not repent.

Three things are taught us in this most remarkable story. Sin brings the sinner under the judgments of God, and a place of power and influence only augments the guilt. A throne and the "divinity which doth hedge a king" cannot stay the chastening hand. A nation led into sin is a doomed nation, and kings must repent like other men.

This thrice blessed truth is found in our story: there is no man too vile for the reach of the everlasting mercy, and no iniquity too deep for pardoning grace. It would seem, in the case of Manasseh, as if God wanted to leave on record a paramount example of His divine compassion, an enduring monument of His saving mercy.

We are also taught that we cannot take our full indulgence of fleshly lusts, and go the full length in our godless ways, and then think that through forgiveness all will be as if it had never been. It teaches us that we must not presume upon pardoning mercy. God has left us this story of the nation that did not come back with its king, and the sad picture of the boy who followed his father's footsteps into the very pit from which his father through infinite mercy escaped. We cannot trifle with sin; there is always death, even the undying death in the fatal cup. The harvest of shame and ruin always follows, even when forgiveness saves the greatest of sinners. Mercy to the uttermost, salvation to the worst of men shines in this record, and along with that the stern fact that sin brings death to some one, even while boundless mercy hears the cry of the mighty transgressor.

Manasseh was saved, but the nation perished and the son was lost. Mercy and judgment go hand in hand, and sin always casts a dark shadow somewhere.

References: II Kings, chapters 20 to 24; II Chronicles 33; Jeremiah 15:4.

Sanballat

THE HINDERER

Some men achieve notoriety—not from anything which they do, but because they get in the way of the fellow who is doing something. Such men never would be heard of, but for the fact that they are a thorn in the flesh of some man or woman who is busy in some great undertaking.

Such an one was Sanballat, the enemy of Jerusalem and the would-be hinderer of Nehemiah. Nehemiah had undertaken a big job; he was building a city, and doing it with discouraged and half-hearted workmen, and under very adverse conditions. Any sort of building is hard work, and the task of Nehemiah was unusually difficult.

Sanballat was perfectly contented, and remained quiet until something was attempted. He was gratified as long as the walls were down and the city had no gates. He would have been delighted to see things even worse than they were. He hated Jerusalem and her people, and rejoiced in their misfortune. However, just as soon as Nehemiah began to rebuild the city he got busy.

The devil will let a church alone until a real revival comes along and his territory is invaded, and then he will begin to show just how mean a devil he is. Every good work has its Sanballat and Tobiah, and the devil is always on hand to help them along. Every man, good or bad, has some one who will boost for him, and Tobiah was a sort of echo of Sanballat. The record says that when the walls of Jerusalem began to be builded, the company of Sanballat were grieved exceedingly. It hurts some people like the toothache to see the cause of righteousness prosper. These folk were jealous of Jerusalem; they rejoiced in its desolation, and it almost killed them to see it being restored.

There are enemies of good who really suffer when the cause of God prospers. The devil is always glad when the walls of Zion crumble, and is sorry when they are rebuilt; and Sanballat and his crowd are legitimate children of his satanic majesty. They were disappointed very much that the city of God should have walls that could not easily be broken down and gates which would keep out the danger. The evil one and his satellites hate a prosperous church, and are troubled greatly by a real revival; it just mortifies that gang to see the saints happy and sinners repenting.

Every good enterprise meets opposition from folk of that character and always will. Sanballat and his company tried to see what they could do with ridicule and derision, for unless people are in downright earnest these are mighty effective weapons. "Just look at those feeble Jews! What do they think they are going to do? Do they think they are able to revolt against the great king of Medo-Persia? Rebuild the walls of that old city! Oh, what a joke!" Nowadays, they will say, "Oh yes, they are going to have a revival in town, going to put the bootleggers out of business, going to try to stop drunkenness! Oh, how funny!" Now all this sort of ridicule is born of fear; deep down in their hearts the cohorts of sin are really afraid that things are going to be done.

The Biggest Coward in the World

There is no bigger coward in all the world than the devil, and no greater expert at running a bluff. Half a dozen real, dead-in-earnest, true-hearted men and women can always put the devil to flight by resisting him and holding forth the shield of faith. Sanballat was fearful that Jerusalem might be restored, and that Nehemiah might succeed, so he said, "Maybe we can laugh them out of it," and they began to belittle what was being done. They said, "The work will amount to nothing; the walls will be worthless; just look at the stones they are using; they have been lying around covered with moss for a hundred years. They think they can build Jerusalem again; just as well try to dam up the Euphrates with straws, or defeat the armies of the great king. We feel sorry for Nehemiah. Poor fellow, he is just wasting his time; it is a pity that he does not know better! If even a little fox should climb upon that wall it would fall down." Then they all tried to laugh and feel big about what they had said.

However, they did not stop the work, and the work never stops where there is a Nehemiah for the leader. The Sanballats talk the same way now; they will say, "All your converts are going to backslide; they won't hold out for a month. Just wait till someone offers that reformed drunkard a drink; and that fellow who was so profane will be cussing again in a little while."

But, the building of the walls went on, and they became very angry. It is a good sign when the devil gets mad; it shows that something is being done which he does not like. Sanballat and his crowd said, "We will stop this thing; if they cannot be laughed out, we will frighten them out; we will use a show of force, and will just bluff them out of it."

However, Nehemiah knew how to deal with that company. He said, "If nothing will do them but a fight we will be ready for it." So the workmen of Nehemiah went to their work with swords by their sides and all their weapons of war within easy reach.

They said in substance, "Just do your worst; we don't want

a fight; we want to rebuild our city; but we believe that the walls or Jerusalem are worth fighting for, and the work will not stop." And it was soon apparent that while the Sanballats and Tobiahs were long on talking, they were short on real warfare, and had poor stomachs for cold steel.

Every effort for building the cause of righteousness, every reform, every effort that undertakes to build the kingdom of God and combat age-old iniquity has met the hate and ridicule of organized sin. Every great accomplishment of real value to humanity has had its soldiers and martyrs. The cause of human slavery had its Sanballats, as well as its Nehemiahs. The old liquor traffic has used every weapon that Sanballat used and is still fighting. The soil of our country has drunk the blood of men whose consciences would not allow them to keep silent. Gambling, drink and the white slave traffic, that foul triumvirate of greed, appetite and lust, have derided, slandered and murdered those who sought to restrain them. Those who jest about the efforts to overthrow these vampires of the race are the folk who deep down in their hearts want them to ravage and hurt our youth unhindered; and if you will inquire closely, you will learn that somewhere along the line they make gain from the foul business.

Sanballat and his confederates said the wall would be worthless when built, that a little fox would break it down. The fact of the matter was they did not believe what they said about it; they would not have been concerned if that had been true. What they really feared was that the wall would be strong and that Jerusalem would be well fortified. The same thing is true today; the fellows who cry that great evils must be let alone because they cannot be regulated or controlled are the fellows who want them to flourish and to carry on their evil work unhindered. The same forces belittle every law which curbs the power of these enemies of society, for the simple reason that they are in full sympathy with their nefarious business.

Friends of Crime Ridicule the Righteous

The friends of unfettered lawlessness spend a great deal of energy ridiculing the men and women who oppose vice and greed as kill-joys, who want to take all the pleasure out of life. The "wet" press everywhere specializes in that sort of stuff, and you will hear in minor tones the approving chatter of the Tobiahs, who feel called upon to sneeze when the Sanballats take snuff.

The hypocritical defender of vice and crime is not pained when children live in rags and filth, and die in dirty and neglected homes; he does not feel any pangs of remorse when women go unkempt and hungry, and are beaten black and blue by drunken husbands; but he becomes vociferous against those who would limit the supply of rum for his debased appetite, and cut off his revenue which comes from the weakness and depravity of his fellows. He wails loudly about "blue laws," and any law that restrains his corrupt activities looks mighty blue.

The Machiavellian insincerity of such men exhausts the range of the English language and the flexibility of the Greek to find words which accurately describe it. They are the Sanballats and Tobiahs who seek to fetter the builders of the New Jerusalem.

Our churches have folk of this ilk. Start something which means progress, sacrificial service, self-denial, or liberality, and you will hear the complaints of the Sanballats and the echoing whine of the Tobiahs. They will hamper the enterprise with inaction and inertia, mutter about expenses, and complain that the sacred traditions of the past are being forgotten.

Sometimes Sanballat becomes a vociferous defender of the truth, broadcasts to the multitudes his heroic devotion to orthodoxy, and contends after a Philistine fashion for the "faith once delivered to the saints." Faith is a treasure beyond price and should be guarded as sedulously as the vestal virgins watched the ever-burning fires, or the Jews kept the ark of the holy covenant; but to make a pretence of reverence for it, in order to be in a position to hamper the work of the kingdom, or to hold a place of leadership among the plain, unsuspecting people of the churches for self-aggrandizement is diabolical. Many a pastor, with his soul aflame for righteousness and the salvation of men, has had his heart crushed and his zeal chilled by the Sanballats who have crept into the church and stolen the vestments of true religion, that they might serve the prince of darkness.

Every road of progress has had its Sanballats and Tobiahs; they snarled at the heels of Washington and the heroes of the Revolution. The cabals formed against that great leader were planned and carried out by men of that spirit. The same tribe made life miserable for Harvey, Jenner, Pasteur, and men of their sort in the field of medicine. They have ridiculed and cheapened every great invention and have been the agelong enemies of progress. Stephenson met them when he invented the locomotive, and Cartright encountered their opposition when he began to weave cloth by machinery. The pioneers of the air, who made aviation possible, faced the scorn of a thousand Sanballats and their servile Tobiahs.

To listen to that crowd and be swayed by them is unworthy of real kingdom builders. They are able to apply heavy pressure at times; social and financial arguments are used; the preacher must shut up or his salary will not be paid; and the business man who stands for righteousness may lose his place and business. Anyone who allows himself to be hushed by such intimidations labels himself as a coward for revenue only.

The Nehemiahs have a big place in history and in the long run they always win. Constructive forces always triumph in the final battle; all that hinderers can do is to make it hard for the builders. The Sanballats are waging a losing fight, and their names get into the records only because they trouble the Nehemiahs. They have notoriety but no fame, and their place in the limelight is short-lived. Many people forget that the everlasting stars fight on the side of truth and progress, and while they may be delayed, they cannot be permanently stopped.

There were plenty of critics when Noah was building the ark, but the faultfinders learned that they had better have spent their time in learning to swim. There were fellows who sat around while Solomon was building the temple and wore out the bosom of their trousers—or whatever men wore in place of trousers those days—but we know none of their names; yet we have all heard of Solomon and Hiram, and the temple belongs to the ages.

Three Classes of Sanballats

We might mention three classes who make up the Sanballats and Tobiahs of earth. There is the venal crowd who are actuated by self-interest only. They are for sale to the highest bidder, and will shout just as loudly for one side as another, if the pay is there. To this crowd belong the supporters of the great moral evils of the world; they are standing by their appetites and purses, and will continue to do so. Like Demetrius, they will shout long and loud for religion when their craft by which they have their wealth is in danger. They are committed to evil because they love it, and because they make money out of it. They make a business of deviltry, and whatever is good and clean is their enemy.

These are the hopeless cases; they have sold out; the price has been paid, and they are delivering the goods. They are mastered by appetite and greed, and they really rejoice in the triumph of the forces of evil. The only hope for them is the renewing grace of God making them new creatures in Christ Jesus.

Some of the clan are just little of soul and narrow of mind; they cannot dream big dreams, or visualize great undertakings. They are in a way sincere in their attitude, but do just as much harm as the outright enemies of right. They are reactionary by nature and training; they want nothing changed; they are immune to new ideas and bigger things. They are like the dog in the manger in the old fable; they cannot eat the hay and they mean to see that no one else does. They snap and bark at the heels of the workers who are building the walls of Zion. These are to be pitied and prayed for, and if possible, taught rather than fought.

Then there are the Sanballats who are the victims of envy and jealousy. The building Nehemiahs have been preferred to them, and they cannot endure to see someone else succeed where they have failed. Their selfish desire for pre-eminence has been thwarted, and their hatred of the bigger man has led them into the way of opposition. They belittle the work of others, and impugn the motives of faithful workers and besmirch their characters. They know every whispered slander and every dirty innuendo about the builders. They whisper; they insinuate; they tell half-truths, and revel in a carnival of suspicion and evil imaginings. The devil is a slanderer according to Holy Writ, and these fellows prove themselves legitimate sons of his satanic majesty. This part, at least, of the Sanballats and Tobiahs has no difficulty in establishing their unroyal descent.

After all, it does not pay to be a hinderer; most of them dwindle out after doing much harm and being a nuisance for a while. Anyone who sees clearly had rather be a "dog and bay the moon" than to attract temporary attention in this way. One monkey cutting capers on a telephone pole, or one thug putting obstructions on the railway track, will get more short-lived notice than the workers building a skyscraper or the engineer driving the train. The monkey will be pleased after his apish fashion, and the thug will get in the morning paper —one time; but the monkey will wind up in a cage, and the criminal behind the bars of some jail. Some people mistake notoriety for fame, and spend their lives in the shadow of their mistake.

The Sanballats have founded no empires and builded no cities; they have established no schools and erected no churches; they have healed no diseases and cast out no demons. They have written no songs, painted no pictures, and carved no immortal statues. They are the mosquitoes and flies that annoy the workers. They are the curs that yelp and snap around the wheels of progress. They are the wild boars which rend and ravage the gardens of industry. Their weapons are ridicule, slander and persecution. They have pestered the Nehemiahs, killed the Pauls, and imprisoned the Galileos; but they have only delayed the good work; they never stopped anything.

It is best, if possible, to ignore them, for few of them are seekers after truth, and most of them are fully inoculated against sound teaching. Pray for them, but keep building walls and swinging gates. If they threaten by force, let them know that goodness does not mean weakness nor cowardice.

Sanballat attracted some transient attention and made an ugly spot on the record, but that was all. Too little and short-sighted to fall in line and help, he is remembered solely because he got in the way of a bigger and better man.

References: Nehemiah, chapters 2, 4 and 6.

David

THE SINNING SAINT

Most of the great characters of sacred history had some distinguishing trait in which they stood out above their fellows. Abraham was great in faith, Moses by his steadfast meekness, Job by his sublime patience which endured all and conquered all. David, however, was pre-eminent in more lines than any other character recorded in the inspired story.

When a shepherd boy he defended his flock just a bit more courageously than other herdsmen about Bethlehem. The sling, the plaything of the other boys, became in his hands a conquering weapon of war. The harp was found in many homes, but no player among them coaxed such exquisite music from its strings.

Bacon said, "Some men are born great, some achieve greatness, and some have greatness thrust upon them." This three-fold excellence belonged to David, the son of Jesse. He was born great, so that all the elements of greatness were inherent in his nature. Few men have been so richly endowed by essential elements as this son of the Judean hills. His birthright was manifold: the soaring genius, the courage that rose to meet emergencies, the princely qualities of leadership, and the magnetism that knit men to him with hooks as it were of steel—all these belonged to his wondrous personality.

He achieved greatness; his exploits were of the highest order. His slaying of Goliath in a time of inaction on the part of the army gave him at once the hearts of Israel. His sudden leap into fame by one daring deed is a fireside story wherever the Bible is read. He was the builder of the Israelitish kingdom. Before David's day, they were a group of loosely-knit tribes; he wove them into an empire. His military campaigns were of high order, and he extended the borders of the nation above any before or after him. He became the national hero. There were thousands of men in Saul's army stronger of body and better armed than he, but they did not slay the Philistine champion and become the idol of the nation. Israel had no other king who was so uniformly victorious over their enemies.

Men like David win victories regardless of equipment; a stone and a sling will do for them what a king's armour will not do for other men. When a man like David comes along, weapons take care of themselves. He was ready for the fray; if the armour of Saul would not do, he could conquer with a shepherd's weapons. The story of David is too long and too full of achievement to be dealt with in a short article.

Greatness was thrust upon him when the nation in a pivotal hour chose him most enthusiastically as its ruler. The whole nation gathered at Hebron, and with great demonstrations crowned him King of all Israel. All these things combined to make the ruddy-cheeked boy, whom Samuel had anointed, one of the very greatest of Israel's illustrious sons. He was the helmsman who steered the people through troubled waters into a place of power and strength—the mighty strategist who repelled their enemies, and brought safety and stability to the hitherto loosely-knit people.

Great Capacity for Friendship

His capacity for friendship was one of the qualities which made men love him and follow him to the death. His friendship for Jonathan flowered in rare beauty athwart the background of hate and suspicion in which it bloomed. The cruel jealousy of Saul, which drove him into exile, shows in vivid contrast with the magnanimity with which he spared his foe when he was delivered into his hands.

His memorial song at the death of Saul and Jonathan reveals the spirit which made his fame enduring. Its divine forgetfulness lends a tragic glory to the name of his bitterest enemy. Only a soul of epic mould could so sorrow the passing of a foe, and such a spirit reveals moral qualities of the highest order. There is an immortal beauty in his tribute to the love of Jonathan, a love "passing the love of women." If David had written nothing else, these lines would have made sure his place in the anthology of song. The story of the three heroes who risked life and limb to bring their beloved leader the water from the well by Bethlehem's gate sets forth the spirit that made him the idol of his followers. He loved and was loved as few men that have ever lived.

Under his leadership, the worship of Jehovah came to its place in the organic life of the state. The glory and majesty of the God of Abraham gripped and mastered the soul of David, and there was no taint of idolatry in his career. He never bowed at any heathen shrine, and he gave to the God of his fathers a whole-hearted devotion unequaled by any other ruler of the chosen people. He so followed the worship of Jehovah that future kings were measured by the degree in which they approximated the faithfulness and loyalty of David. To say that one walked in the way of David was the loftiest encomium which could be placed upon any of his successors. He marked out the way of obedience and righteousness, as Jeroboam the son of Nebat traced the course of sin and death. The worship of David was not the heartless and soulless formalism which cursed the latter days of the Jewish people, but the real hunger after God which marked the high hours of the true prophets of Israel.

A Great Poet

David was a poet of the first order, and in a more gifted age would have lifted Hebrew literature to the first place in the eyes of history. All that has come to us from his pen are his spiritual songs which have never been surpassed. Possibly no poem in the long roll of such productions has gripped the heart of the world like the Twenty-third Psalm. Its simple yet profound words speak the language of the heart and express the experiences of a soul which has sought and found the rest which is the goal of seeking humanity. The saints of all time have found no words to fit their hours of ecstatic joy better than those of the One hundred third Psalm. In it the words of praise and reverential delight reached the high tides of the expressions of real sainthood. The Fifty-first Psalm is the classic of penitence and contrite confession for the ages.

In psalms like these and in the majestic faith of the Forty-sixth Psalm, along with the vision of God in nature shown by the Nineteenth Psalm, are revealed the soaring genius of David when kindled by holy encounters with the realities of the spiritual life. David's piety is shown here as nowhere else, and his inner life was built upon the recognition of the heinousness of his sin and God's merciful forgiveness.

The deep understanding of the guilt of his transgression and the abhorrence of the thing which had dragged him down are found in the words of David, as in the words of no other. It is the baseness of his sin which sears his very soul and shames him into the dust. His cry is not for deliverance from punishment, but from the sense of defilement which makes him condemn himself. If David had no other claim to greatness, he would be known as the man who had most fully understood and told of the degradation of sin, and the blessed estate of him "whose transgression is forgiven, whose sin is covered."

Great Love for Music

David loved music and brought it into its place in the worship of Jehovah. His glorious psalms were, most of them, written for the temple worship and were sung by the choirs he established. A study of the services which he arranged for the tabernacle shows most elaborate musical programs. He was himself a musician of no mean ability. It was the harp of David which broke the gloom and dissipated the shadows which gathered around the closing days of defeated Saul. Byron, in his "Hebrew Melodies," says of him:

"The harp the monarch minstrel swept,
   The King of men beloved of Heaven,
Which Music hallow'd while she wept
   O'er tones her heart of hearts had given,
   Redoubled be her tears, its chords are riven!
It soften'd men of iron mould,
   It gave them virtues not their own;
No ear so dull, no soul so cold,
   That felt not, fired not to the tone
   Till David's lyre grew mightier than his throne.

It told the triumphs of our King,
   It wafted glory to our God;
It made our gladden'd valleys ring,
   The cedars bow, the mountains nod;
   Its sound aspired to heaven and there abode!
Since then, though heard on earth no more,
   Devotion and her daughter Love
Still bid the bursting spirit soar
   To sounds that seem as from above,
   In dreams that day's broad light cannot remove."

David's Greatest Sin

David was a man of strong passions and his deepest sins were of that nature. His anger flamed forth in deeds which in the light of our day seems barbarous and cruel. Sins of love and lust cursed his life and shadowed its closing days. His home was that of the polygamous rulers of his day, and he put no restraints upon the appetites of the flesh. His adultery with the wife of Uriah and the murder of her gallant husband stand out black and ugly in the record of his life. It seems hard to reconcile some of these things with the lofty spiritual aspirations of many of his psalms. This much may be said in palliation, the virtues of David were far beyond the day in which he lived, and his sins were the everyday deeds of the monarchs all about him. To take the life of any man who stood in their way, to possess the person of any woman who appealed to their carnal lusts was the almost universal custom of oriental despots.

It may well be said of David that his faults were those of his age, and his virtues immeasurably above his surroundings. God, however, did not allow these considerations to mitigate his punishment, nor did David in the hour of his contrition make any such claim. His penitence was sincere, and his sorrow deep and pungent. Those who wonder at the approval of God upon a life which had such black pages must see not only his heinous sins, but also his abject humiliation and the poignant cry for mercy in order to understand. God had no leniency for his sin, but He understood the true repentance which turned from it with loathing and horror.

Another weakness in the life of David was his failure to check the evils which arose in his home. We have already mentioned his polygamous marriages which brought their customary heritage of trouble. Not only would there be discord in such a home, but David seemed to feel that his children were above the laws which regulate ordinary humanity. The foul sins of Ammon which went unpunished and the cruel revenge and rebellion of Absalom must have brought measureless sorrow to David. These sins which grew out of the curse of polygamy blighted his house and left a dark shadow upon his posterity.

"Your Sin Will Find You Out"

In this wonderful life we see the law of the harvest working to its uttermost. God loved David and Israel too well to allow his sin to go unchastened. Greatness has no exemption clause in the judgments of the Almighty, and glorious experiences and memorable service will not hold back His smiting hands from sinning saints. Greatness makes big blunders, as well as it achieves dazzling successes. The same souls that soar to heavenly heights sometimes explore the nether depths.

God said to David by the lips of Nathan, the hero prophet, "Therefore the sword shall never depart from thine house; because thou has despised me, and hast taken the wife of Uriah the Hittite to be thy wife. Thus saith the LORD, Behold, I will raise up evil against thee out of thine own house, and I will take thy wives before thine eyes, and give them unto thy neighbor, . . . for thou didst it secretly: but I will do this thing before all Israel, and before the sun" (II Sam. 12:10–12). How that dire sentence must have echoed in the soul of David when he learned of the shame of Ammon, and his death at the hands of his revengeful brother! What an agony of remorse awoke as he listened to the tragic word from the thick-boughed oak and the heap of stones in the wood of Ephraim!

All the tragedies of Shakespeare, the master dramatist, fall short of the somber picture of the aged king, staggering to that room over the gate at Mahanaim, wailing out as he went,

"O my son Absalom, my son, my son Absalom! would God I had died for thee, O Absalom, my son, my son!" No painter of all time has limned such a portrait as the inspired penman has left us of this desolate monarch, crushed by the ripening of his sin. In no life of all history has there been written more indelibly the truth that "the wages of sin is death."

A Sinner Saved By Grace

There is no discounting the greatness of David. He was cast in a big pattern, and his life was keyed to a lofty pitch. Great, even in the sports of boyhood, dazzling the multitude by his youthful heroism, he gleams upon the records of Israel. The days of his outlawry are aglow with deeds of daring, as well as acts of magnanimity and chivalry. The years of sovereignty were marked by conquest and statesmanship. His zeal for Jehovah, his clear concepts of holiness, and his deep spiritual experiences stamp him as one of the heaven-born leaders of the religious world. His poetic genius and seraphic imagination abide in the heart messages of his wonderful psalms.

It would seem as if God wanted to show His people, through the example of David, that the loftiest sainthood does not save them from temptations, nor free them from the laws of retribution. Intensely human, versatile in gifts, courageous and magnanimous, resplendent in imagination, rich in spiritual life, ugly and sensual in his sins, he stands before us. He was manly in his saintliness, and saintly in his virile manhood. His psalms thrill us, while his transgressions startle us. His words of seraphic heavenliness woo us, while his sins repel us. To know David we must know his reckless daring, his faithful friendships, his kingly rule, his military ability, his hours of inspiration, his fleshly temptations, his tragic fall, and his bitter and sorrowful repentance.

Worn out by his strenuous life, tired of the burdens which

his mistakes had heaped upon him, David went from the shadows of sin to the refuge of the everlasting mercy. He holds his place in the drama of God's unfolding purposes, revealing to us the heights to which a sinner may be raised and the depths to which a saint may sink. Only those may claim a like place who have triumphed with his valor, worshiped with his fervor, praised with his holy ecstacy, sinned with his abandon, and repented with his deep contrition.

He is known as the Shepherd King, as the Sweet Singer of Israel, and as the man after God's own heart; but he still holds the title of the Sinning Saint.

References: I Samuel, chapters 17 to 20; II Samuel, chapters 11, 12, 13; Psalm 51.

Caleb

A PURITAN OF THE LONG AGO

CALEB is one of the virile men of the old Book. See him marching at the head of his clan! Head up, eyes like an eagle, girdle tight, step quick and firm, hair streaming in the wind!

Caleb was not of pure Hebrew blood. The record says that he was a Kenite, and the Kenites were nomadic blacksmiths of no definite nationality. At some time his family, either by adoption or marriage, was numbered with the children of Israel, and Caleb who was only in part of the blood of Abraham became the noblest Hebrew of them all.

We are not told how the family from which Caleb sprang became believers in Jehovah, but Caleb experienced a genuine transformation of life and character. He was a brawny wielder of hammer and file, who loved to hear the ring of his anvil and see the sparks fly from the white iron over his sooty shop. One day the idea of the eternal Jehovah—just, holy and merciful—gripped the heart of this sinewy beater of iron, and he was God's own man. Faith in God became a very real thing to this sturdy blacksmith, and his character became tough and enduring, like the metal that he smelted or the sword blades which he made.

Caleb the Kenite—Caleb the adopted son of Judah—Caleb the convert! The tribe of Judah claimed him; Caleb looked like a good soldier and Judah was ever a fighting tribe. Caleb was anxious for Canaan, and when they wanted twelve spies Caleb likely volunteered; at least, he was the choice of Judah for the dangerous task. He had the spirit of the true pioneer. He could tramp all day, sleep on the ground, and be the first man up in the morning.

I like to picture Caleb as he climbed the hills of the promised country—looking, looking, looking—shading those keen eyes with his hand. Nothing escaped him! He saw the hills and the valleys, the brooks and the springs, the olive orchards and vineyards, and the fig trees laden with fruit. He saw the fields where the wheat and barley grew, and his heart swelled big as he thought how Jehovah had given them such a land. He gazed upon the cities with their massive walls, and counted the layers of masonry, one, two, three, four, all the way to the top. He looked at their soldiers as they passed by, saw just how big they were, and listened to their armour clink. He viewed them over and picked out the place where his sword might find the joints of their coats of mail.

Caleb wanted to raise a war cry and scale those walls, and he could hardly keep from trying his toughened muscles with one of those sons of Anak. Caleb did not believe all that he had heard of their martial prowess. A regular old Puritan image-smasher was Caleb, and his soul blazed with holy indignation as he saw their temples filled with idols and beheld the obscene orgies of their worship. He was not afraid of any crowd who worshiped a piece of painted wood, prayed to a polished stone, or put their faces in the dust before a metal image that he could knock to pieces with his old hammer. Caleb said, "I am not afraid of men who worship things like these, no matter how big they are or what sort of walls they hide behind." Caleb had the royal imagination of the true believer; he had heard Jehovah speak at Sinai, and had followed the fiery pillar through the desert; he saw dead giants and crumbling walls, and heard the rams' horns of Israel sounding the note of victory.

Majority Report of the Spies

It was a mighty interesting time when the spies returned to make their report. Caleb was anxious to take Canaan, and if there was to be any fighting he was ready. He was amazed as he listened to the ten tell about what they had seen and how they felt. They said the land was all right, a wonderful place; but they had a frightful story of walled cities whose towers reached to the heavens, and gigantic soldiers in whose presence they felt like grasshoppers. Now Caleb did not feel like a grasshopper; he stood there beside Joshua and wanted to stop the mouths of those whining cowards. It had never for one moment entered his mind that the host of Israel would listen to that crowd of weaklings; he judged things by his own intrepid spirit.

Like many committees, the spies brought in a majority and minority report. The majority report said the land was just what they had been promised, but they were scared and their fear colored the report. They had forgotten nearly everything, except how badly panic-stricken they were. Terror and cowardice are as contagious as measles, and break out much more quickly. All the host of Israel began to have visions of walls whose tops were hidden by the clouds, and of mighty giants in glittering armour. They began to wish that they were back in Egypt making brick; and some of them even wished that they were dead, so they could not be frightened any more.

Caleb brought in the minority report, and it sounds just like him:—"Let us go up at once, and possess it; for we are well able to overcome it." "At once . . . possess it . . . well able. . ."; in these words we have the measure of the spirit of Caleb. Caleb was no orator—his sort seldom are. He saw the tide was against him, so he gritted his teeth, clenched his fist and walked off to his tent. Will he give up and die? Not a bit of it; such men don't die easily. I think I hear him saying, "I am going into Canaan; I am going to help take those towns; and I am not going to die until I whip those giants."

"But think of forty years in the desert! Caleb, you will be dead before Israel ever crosses Jordan!"

"Not I," said Caleb; "my job is not finished till those giants are dead."

Tramp, tramp, tramp over rocks and sands, moving tents, herding sheep, camels and goats; mighty tame work for a man who wanted to conquer Canaan and slay giants. One day the news came that one of the spies was dead and Caleb went to the funeral. Another died, and Caleb and Joshua were among the pallbearers. The poor fellows were dying—scared to death by the giants whom they had not seen for twenty years! The last one died, and Caleb helped to lower his body into the sand; but his hands did not tremble, and no one thought of him as an old man.

If you had listened down where the blacksmith's tent stood, you might have heard the music of his hammer—clink, clank, clatter. Caleb was making swords, sharpening spear-heads, shaping armours, getting ready to go over Jordan. You might have seen him making plows, mattocks and pruning hooks. Somebody said, "What do you mean, Caleb? there is no farming here in the desert."

"Of course not," said Caleb; "I am just getting ready to farm in Canaan."

Caleb Survives the Ten Spies

Forty years slipped away, and not a grown man was alive who had crossed the Red Sea, save Joshua and Caleb. All dead—every murmurer dead—every doubter dead—all the cowards dead! Who said, "The good die young"? It is false! Weaklings, sissies and cowards die young! True goodness has red blood in its veins. Good men have broad shoulders and a high head. The virtue that counts in this world of evil has hard muscles, a stiff spine and looks the devil squarely in the eye. Some people mistake harmlessness for goodness, and softness for piety. The idolaters did not say, "Dear old Caleb, he hasn't an enemy in the world," and then build their altars next door to his tent; they knew better. They did something more complimentary than patronize Caleb; they respected and feared him.

The goodness that never made an enemy never made anything else. It never promoted a mission; it never fostered a reformation; it never cast out a demon in all the tides of history. Slavery would still traffic in human flesh, lust would seize its victims unafraid, and saloons and gambling hells would have an endless picnic were it not for the Calebs.

Perhaps some kindly soul suggested that Caleb had better retire:—"Let the boys run the shop and you take life easy; you have worked long enough!" Retire? What a word! It has rust in it! It is full of rheumatism, and all sorts of aches and pains! It sounds of rocking chairs, soft cushions and sofa pillows. Put Caleb on the shelf? Put Paul on the list of the superannuated? Retire Stonewall Jackson on half pay before the war is over? There wouldn't be any shelf; if there were, the fellow who undertook the task of retiring Caleb would need it. Moses was dead; Aaron was dead; Miriam was numbered among the departed; but Caleb still tramped through the camp, a regular Hebrew Cato. The anvil rang all day under his sturdy blows, and there was no abating of his virile energy.

We're going over Jordan! What a thrill swept through those desert-bred warriors! The cowards were dead; Caleb was not going to be lonesome this time. You might have seen the old war horse polishing his armour, whetting his sword, or putting a new shaft on his spear head. Is Caleb going with the army? Yes, he is going and not in the commissary department either. He is not pleading his age as an exemption from service, or asking for a seat in one of the baggage wagons.

When they crossed over Jordan, Caleb was one of the first to step in; the old blacksmith headed the fighting men of Judah, the mightiest of the tribes. I think that many a half-hearted soldier was shamed and inspired by his intrepid spirit. He was an example of courage to the whole army.

Caleb Crosses Jordan to Conquer Canaanites

Over Jordan and into Canaan, and the two livest men in the host of Israel were those two octogenarians, Joshua and Caleb. Old? No! Age is not counted by clock ticks, moon changes, and solar revolutions. Age is measured by the springs of life. When they run dry, men are old at thirty or forty. While they keep running, men are young at a hundred. Old? Get a picture of Joshua galloping down the lines, marshalling Israel for a battle! Is Caleb old? Ask someone who marched with him all day, or kept by his side while his sword made a path through the ranks of the enemy.

The conquest was nearly over; the cities and the plains were in the hands of Israel, while back in the mountains lurked the bravest and hardiest of the foe. One day Caleb walked into the tent of Joshua and sat down with his sword across his knees. . "What now, old comrade?" asked Joshua.

"Well," said Caleb, "I have been thinking about those giants up there in the mountains; you know that they scared our people almost to death forty-five years ago. I said then that we could drive them out, but it has not been done; so I have come to ask you to give me as my inheritance the place where they live, and I will go up there and finish them."

"My brother, you are getting old; let some younger man have that job."

You might have seen the flash in Caleb's eyes, as he replied:—"I am eighty-five years old, but I can march just as far and strike just as hard as the day we crossed the Red Sea. Just let me try!" Eighty-five, and asking for the hardest fight in the whole campaign! Who said that men ought to be chloroformed at sixty? It would have been interesting to see the ether squad at Caleb's tent. The fearful were all gone, the doubters were dust, and Caleb was asking for a chance at the giants who scared them to death. Where is the dead line? Caleb never found it; men like him don't find it! Death could not catch, much less kill Elijah; God had to take him to heaven alive.

Up, up, up the mountains! Who are those fellows? Don't they know the Anakim are up there?"

"Oh, that is Caleb and his company!"

"Well, that is another story; there is some fight ahead."

Some days later another company of Israelites timidly followed; at least, they would try to bury the old fellow's bones. Everything was mighty quiet; there were no giants to be seen anywhere! What was that clattering and banging just over the hill? Old Caleb had set up his anvil, had sharpened all the swords and spears lest some other giants might come along, and now he was fixing plows and other implements of husbandry. Caleb had come to stay; at last the old man had settled down.

We don't know when Caleb died, for the historians got tired of waiting and forgot to tell us. Somewhere along the line Caleb went to heaven and Israel was the poorer. What a man! What a figure! It is a pity that Carlyle did not know that period of Bible history a little better. What a hero he would have made out of this fighting, praying blacksmith!

His faith was real; no doubting, no explaining away the super-natural, no trouble about miracles. He believed that God was going to give them the land of Canaan and that He wanted him to fight for it. He believed in God, in the omnipotent Jehovah, and that when He promised something that very thing was coming.

There was no compromise with idols, no looking for good in the rites of the heathen. Stern old Puritan of the Exodus; how he would have delighted to have been with Luther at Worms! Caleb might not have understood all the fine points of theology, but Luther would have had good company. John Knox would have loved him like a brother, and John Bunyan would have enjoyed a visit from him in that Bedford jail. Caleb would have made a wonderful captain to lead a psalm-singing charge with Cromwell's godly Ironsides. The Calebs have been the pioneers of every good cause. They are the never-quits, the die-hards, the uncompromisers of the armies of righteousness.

Caleb would not have been at home in a palace; he would have cut a mighty sorry figure in a drawing room; he would not have fitted in at social receptions and pink teas; but he was a mighty good man to have about when the giants were threatening and cowards were trembling.

The biggest thing about Caleb was his faith in God. When he was converted, he burned all the bridges behind him. He lost his zest for the onions, the leeks and the flesh pots of Egypt. If he were a pastor today, he would not be popular with the dancing, card-playing, cheap show-loving church members, but he would be a mighty good man to hold a revival at Hell's half acre, or lead a fight against the boot-leggers and the red-light gang.

Wholly following Jehovah! He had moral muscle—no easy, slack-twisted theology for him; nothing of this idea that one religion is as good as another. He believed that one was good and all others were false. No heathen altars were built up there in the mountains while Caleb lived. When anyone saw them there he did not need to ask, "Is Caleb dead?" He was head of the house while he lived, and when he laid down the job they sent for the undertaker.

Tough old hero! Worthy beater of iron! His place is in the Hebrew Valhalla! Chief of the old guard, he would die but not surrender; it was the other fellow who died.

This loose-thinking and looser-living age needs just a bit of the iron which was in Caleb's blood. Such men never die; they pass through death but it does not wither them, and life here or hereafter never grows stale. *Caleb is still young in heaven!*

References: Numbers, chapters 13, 14; 26:63–65; 32:10–12; Joshua 14:6–15; 15:13–19.